RECORDED VERSIONS GUITAR

**AUTHENTIC TRANSCRIPTIONS
WITH NOTES AND TABLATURE**

**Transcribed By
JESSE GRESS**

The Beatles / 1967-1970

ISBN 0-7935-3457-7

**HAL•LEONARD™
CORPORATION**

7777 W. BLUEMOUND RD. P.O. BOX 13819 MILWAUKEE, WI 53213

The Beatles / 1967-1970

Strawberry Fields Forever

Words and Music by John Lennon and Paul McCartney

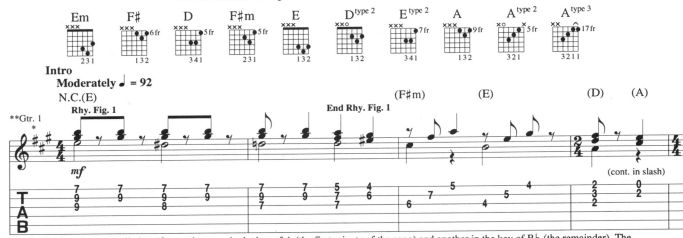

* This song is a compilation of two takes, one in the key of A (the first minute of the song) and another in the key of Bb (the remainder). The difference in keys was compensated for by speeding up the first take and slowing down the second, though this match is not exact.

** Mellotron arr. for gtr.

* tuned down 1 1/2 steps: ⑥ = C# ⑤ = F# ④ = B ③ = E ② = G# ① = C#
Music notated in sounding pitches.

* Gtr. 3 tuned down 1/2 steps: ⑥ = C# ⑤ = F# ④ = B ③ = E ② = G# ① = C#
Music notated in sounding pitches.

*Chorus

Gtr. 1 tacet

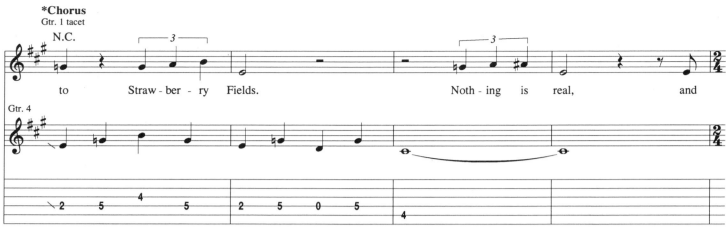

to Straw - ber - ry Fields.   Noth - ing is real,   and

* At this point all gtrs. are arr. to remain in the Key of A

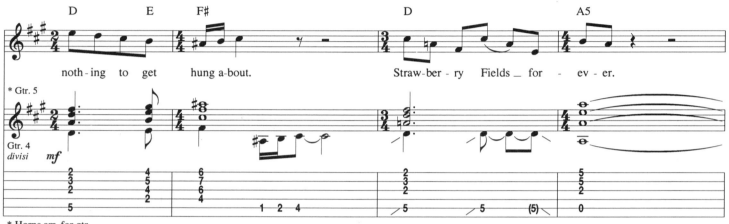

noth - ing to get   hung a-bout.   Straw-ber - ry Fields _ for - ev - er.

* Horns arr. for gtr.

Verse

Gtr. 4 tacet

Gtr. 6: w/ Fill 2

2. No one, I think, is in my tree. _   I mean it must _ be high or

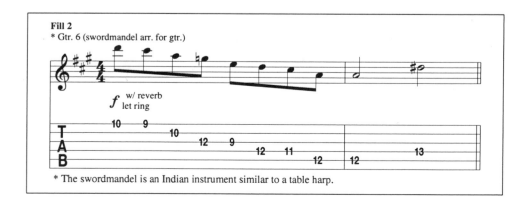

Fill 2
* Gtr. 6 (swordmandel arr. for gtr.)

* The swordmandel is an Indian instrument similar to a table harp.

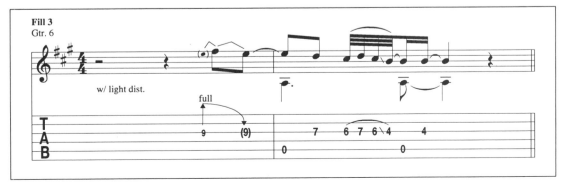

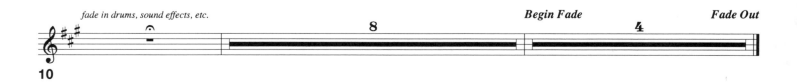

Penny Lane

Words and Music by John Lennon and Paul McCartney

Sgt. Pepper's
Lonely Hearts Club Band

Words and Music by John Lennon and Paul McCartney

Interlude

Gtrs. 1, 2, & 3 tacet

* French horn arr. for gtr.

Chorus

let me in-tro-duce to you, ___ the one and on-ly Bil-ly Shears, ___ and

Ser - geant Pep-per's Lone - ly Hearts_ Club Band, _____ yeah.

Segue into "With A Little Help From My Friends"

With A Little Help From My Friends

Words and Music by John Lennon and Paul McCartney

* French Horn arr. for gtr.

Lucy In The Sky With Diamonds

Words and Music by John Lennon and Paul McCartney

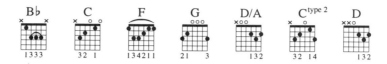

Intro
Moderately ♩ = 124

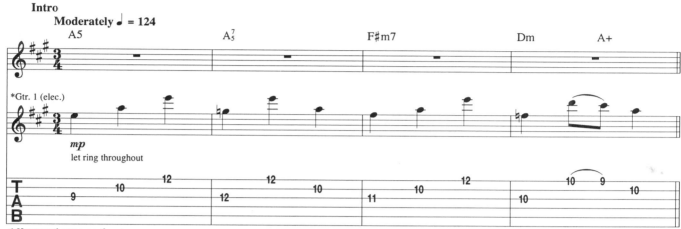

*Gtr. 1 (elec.)

mp
let ring throughout

* Hammond organ arr. for gtr.

Verse

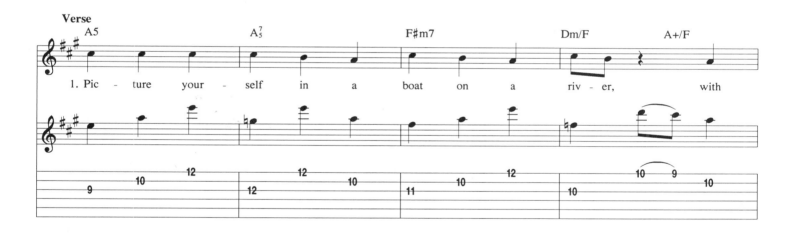

1. Pic - ture your - self in a boat on a riv - er, with

tan - ger - ine trees and mar - ma - lade skies.

Pre-Chorus

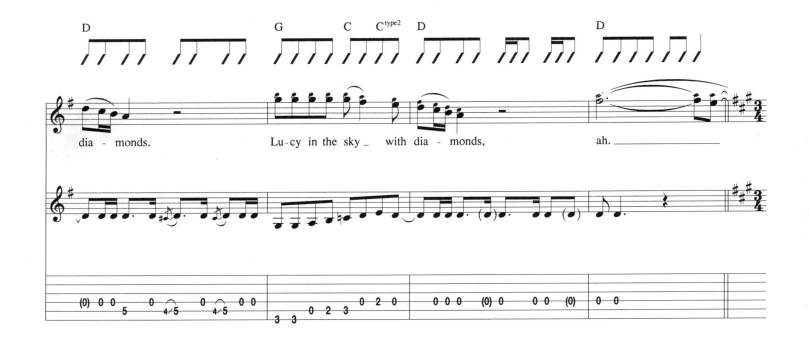

dia - monds.   Lu-cy in the sky __ with dia - monds,   ah. _____

Verse

Gtrs. 2 & 3 tacet

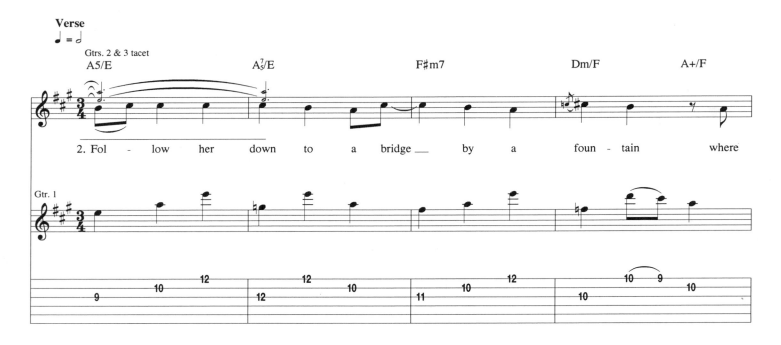

2. Fol - low   her   down   to   a   bridge ___   by   a   foun - tain   where

Gtr. 1

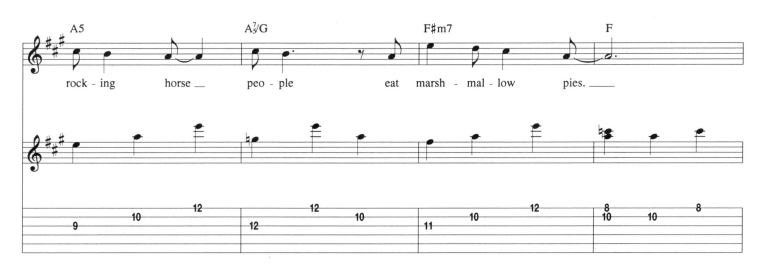

rock - ing   horse ___   peo - ple   eat   marsh - mal - low   pies. ___

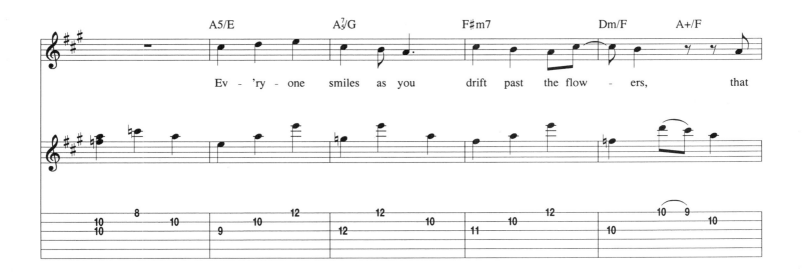

Ev - 'ry - one smiles as you drift past the flow - ers, that

grow so in - cred - i - bly high. _____

Pre-Chorus
Gtr. 1 tacet

News - pa - per tax - is ap - pear _____ on the shore, _____

wait - ing to take _____ you a - way.

Climb in the back with your head in the clouds _____ and you're _____ gone.

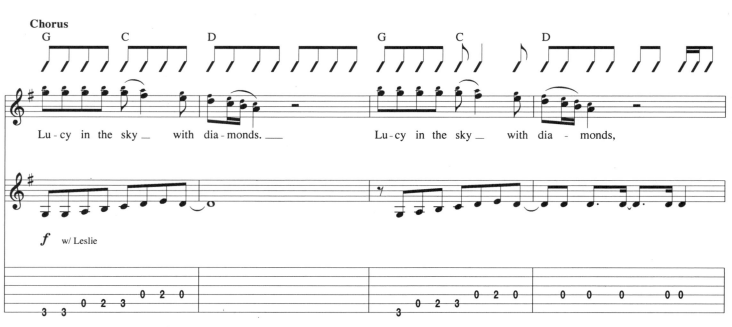

Chorus

Lu - cy in the sky _____ with dia - monds. _____ Lu - cy in the sky _____ with dia - monds,

f w/ Leslie

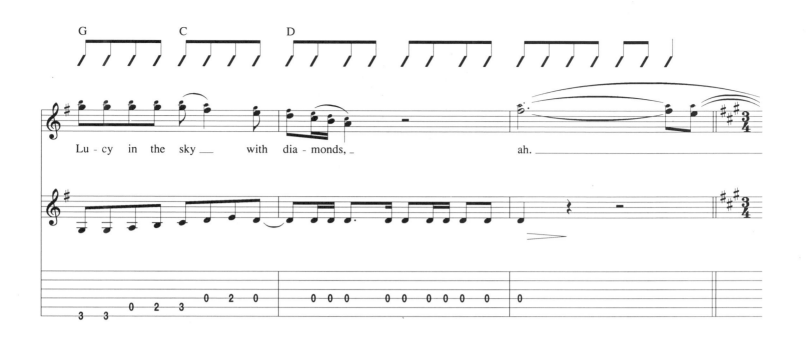

Lu - cy in the sky ___ with dia - monds, ___ ah. ___

Verse

Gtrs. 2 & 3 tacet

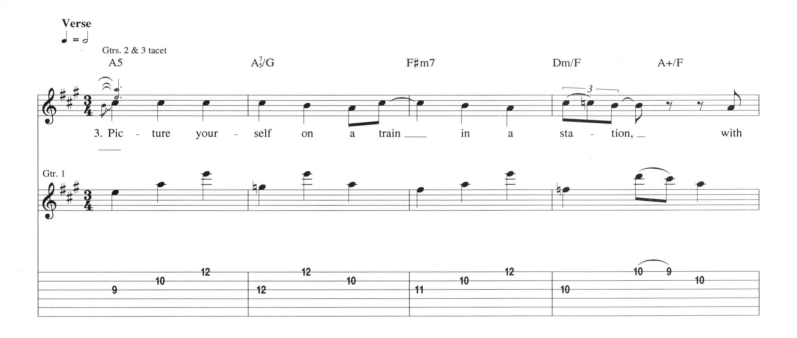

3. Pic - ture your - self on a train ___ in a sta - tion, ___ with

Gtr. 1

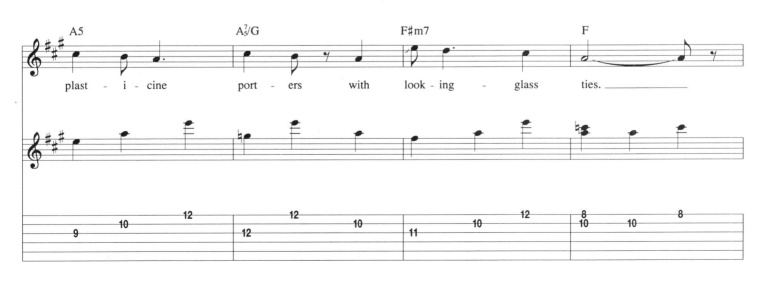

plast - i - cine port - ers with look - ing - glass ties. ___

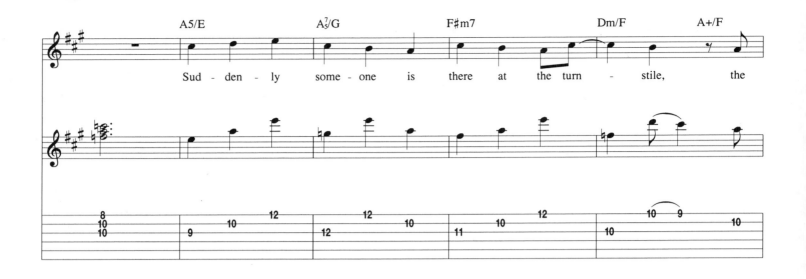

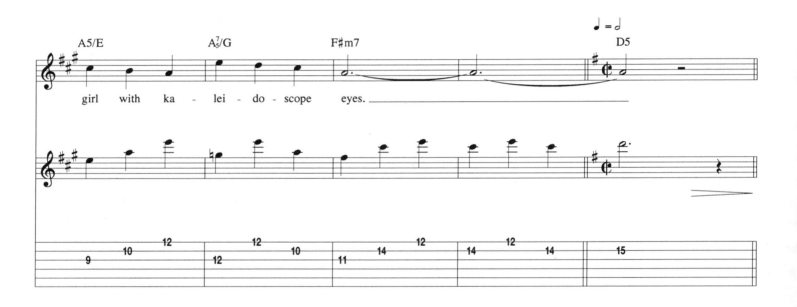

dia - monds, _____ ah. _____

Lu - cy in the sky ___ with dia - monds. ___ Lu - cy in the sky ___ with

Fade Out

dia - monds. ___ Lu - cy in the sky ___ with dia - monds. ___

40

A Day In The Life

Words and Music by John Lennon and Paul McCartney

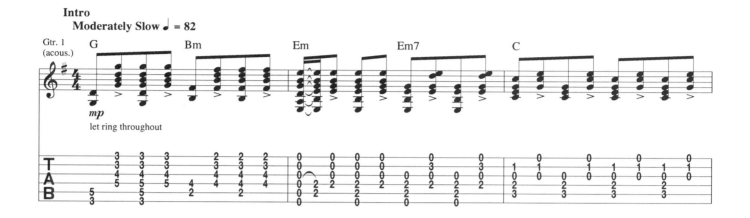

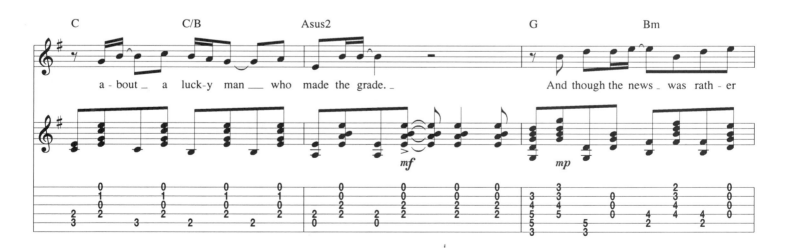

A crowd _ of peo-ple stood and stared. They'd seen his face be-fore. _
A crowd _ of peo-ple turned a - way. But, I just had to look, _

1.

No-bod - y was real - ly sure if he was from the House of Lords. _

2.

hav - ing read the book. _ I'd love to

Orchestral Interlude
Double-Time ♩ = 164
Gtr. 1 tacet
N.C.

turn _ you _ on. _

Spoken: Four, five,

six, sev - en, (etc.)

ah,

ah,

ah.

Verse
Double-Time ♩ = 164

4. I read the news ___

___ to - day, ___ oh boy.

Gtr. 1

mp

Four thou - sand holes ___ in Black - burn, Lan - ca - shire. ___

mf

And though the holes ___ were rath - er

mp

All You Need Is Love

Words and Music by John Lennon and Paul McCartney

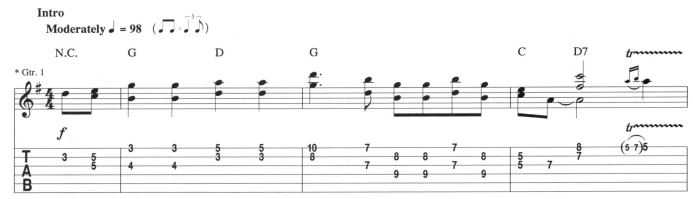

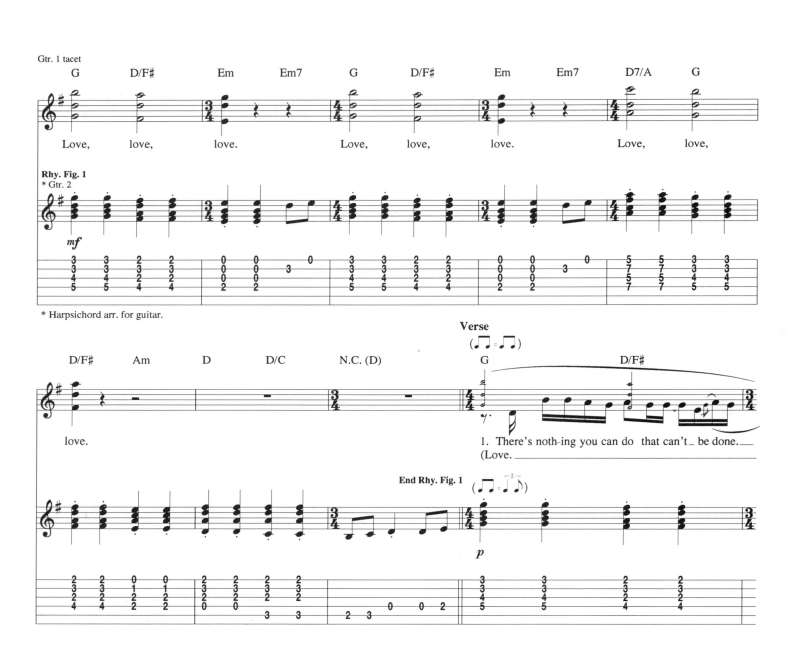

I Am The Walrus

Words and Music By John Lennon And Paul McCartney

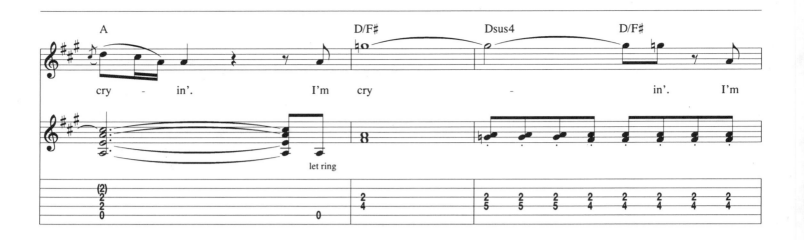

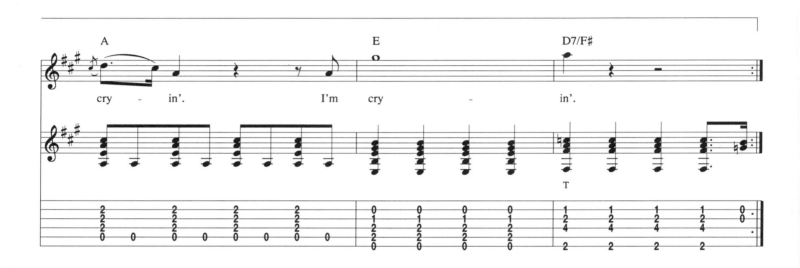

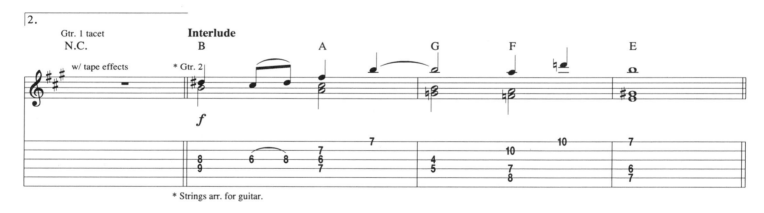

* Strings arr. for guitar.

come you get your tan from stand-ing in the Eng-lish rain.___ I am the

Chorus

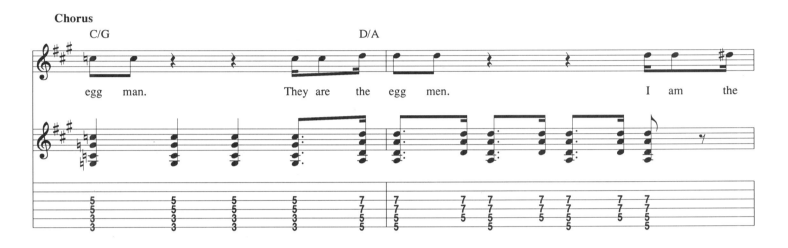

egg man. They are the egg men. I am the

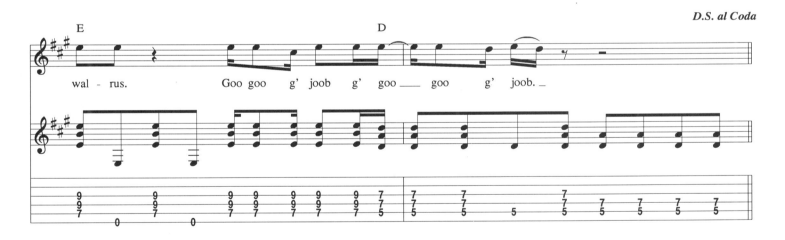

D.S. al Coda

wal - rus. Goo goo g' joob g' goo ___ goo g' joob. ___

⊕ Coda

wal - rus. ___ Goo goo g' joob g' goo ___ goo g' joob.

Outro

Play 4 Times And Fade
(w/ad lib vocals and tape effects)

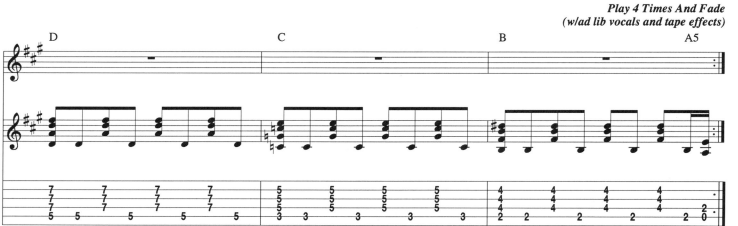

Hello, Goodbye

Words and Music by John Lennon and Paul McCartney

The Fool On The Hill

Words and Music by John Lennon and Paul McCartney

Intro
Slowly ♩ = 72

Verse

1. Day af - ter day,_____ a - lone on a hill,_____ the
2. Well on the way,_____ head in a cloud,_____ the

Rhy. Fig. 1

* Gtr. 1
mf let ring throughout

Gtr. 2 (12-str. acous.)
mf tacet 1st time

* Piano arr. for guitar.

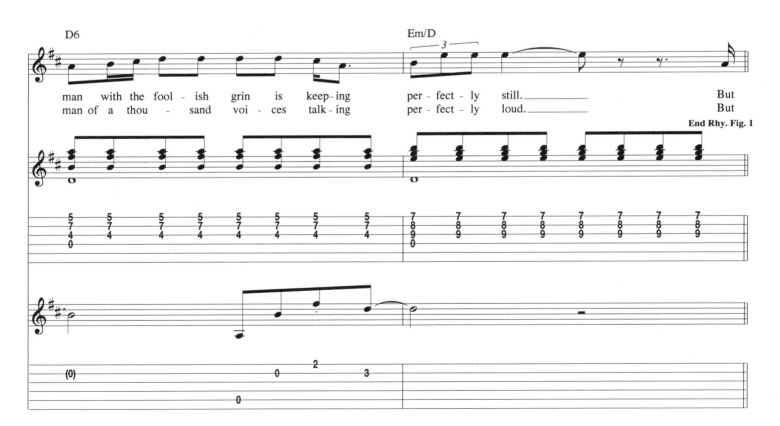

man with the fool - ish grin is keep - ing per - fect - ly still._____ But
man of a thou - sand voi - ces talk - ing per - fect - ly loud._____ But

End Rhy. Fig. 1

Magical Mystery Tour

Words and Music by John Lennon and Paul McCartney

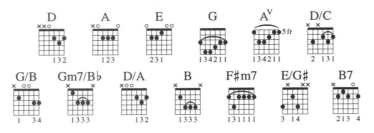

Spoken: Roll up! Roll up for the magical mystery tour. Step right this way!

Roll up, __
(to make a re - ser - va - tion. __)
roll up __ for the mys - ter - y tour.

Chorus
Half - Time Feel

The mag - i - cal mys - ter - y tour is wait - ing to take you a - way,
wait - ing to take you a - way.

2. Roll up, __

roll up __ for the mys - ter - y tour. __
Roll up, __

roll up __ for the mys - ter - y tour. __
Roll up, __
(We've got

67

Lady Madonna

Words and Music by John Lennon and Paul McCartney

*Chord symbols implied by piano.

*2nd and 3rd times

Hey Jude

Words and Music by John Lennon and Paul McCartney

Revolution

Words and Music by John Lennon and Paul McCartney

*Fuzztone results from overloading the mixing console input.
†Notes tabbed at 2nd fret played as open strings.

*Tie 1st time only.

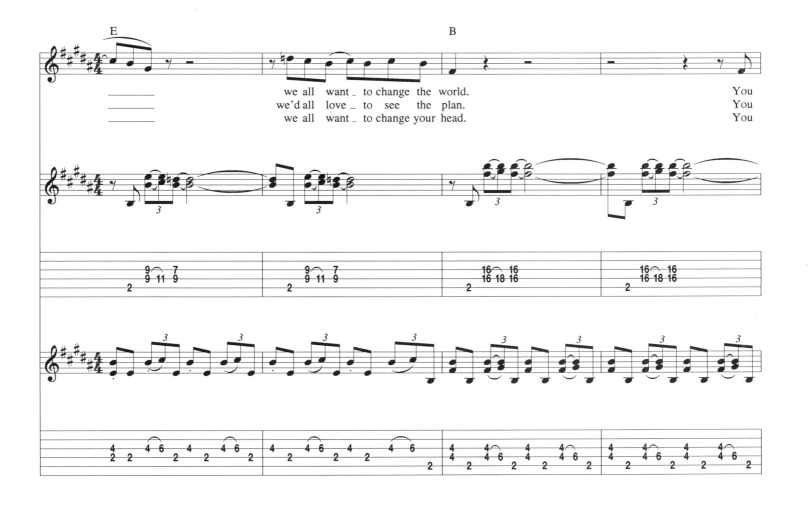

we all want _ to change the world.
we'd all love _ to see the plan.
we all want _ to change your head.

You
You
You

tell me that it's ev-o-lu-tion,_____ well,_____ you know,__
ask me for a con-tri-bu-tion,_____ well,_____ you know,__
tell me it's the in-sti-tu-tion,_____ well,_____ you know,__

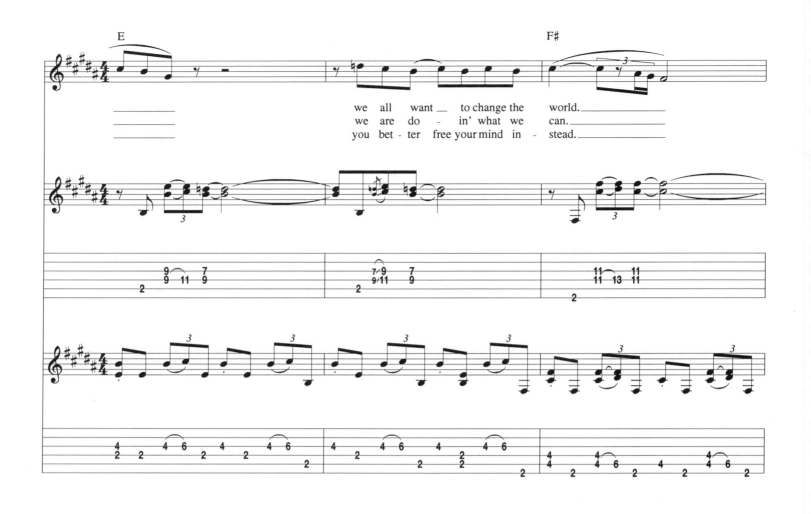

we all want __ to change the world._____
we are do - in' what we can._____
you bet - ter free your mind in - stead._____

Pre - Chorus

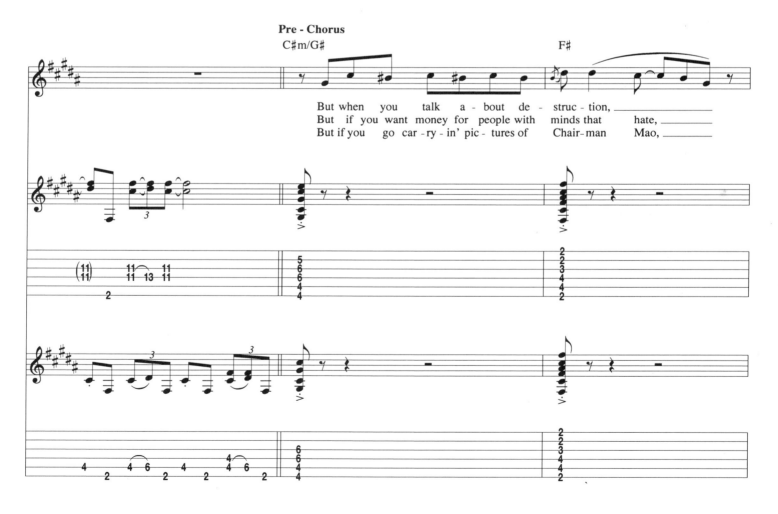

But when you talk a - bout de - struc - tion, _____
But if you want money for people with minds that hate, _____
But if you go car - ry - in' pic - tures of Chair - man Mao, _____

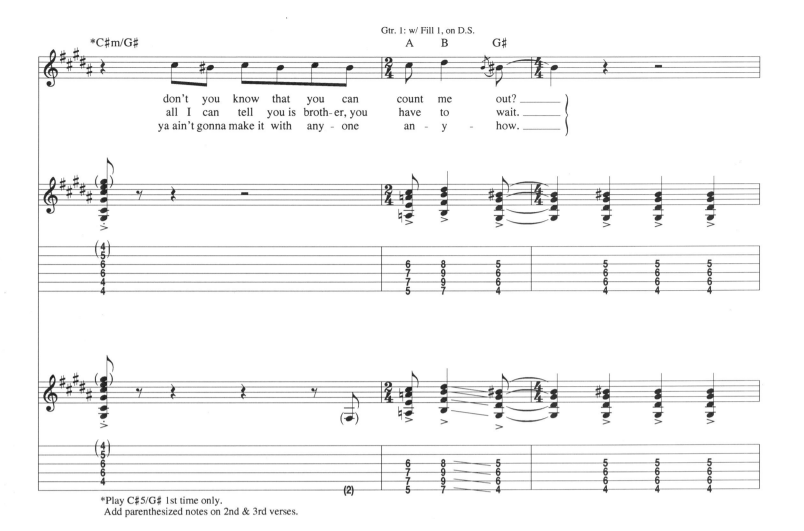

don't you know that you can count me out? _____

all I can tell you is broth-er, you have to wait. _____

ya ain't gonna make it with any - one an - y - how. _____

*Play C#5/G# 1st time only.
Add parenthesized notes on 2nd & 3rd verses.

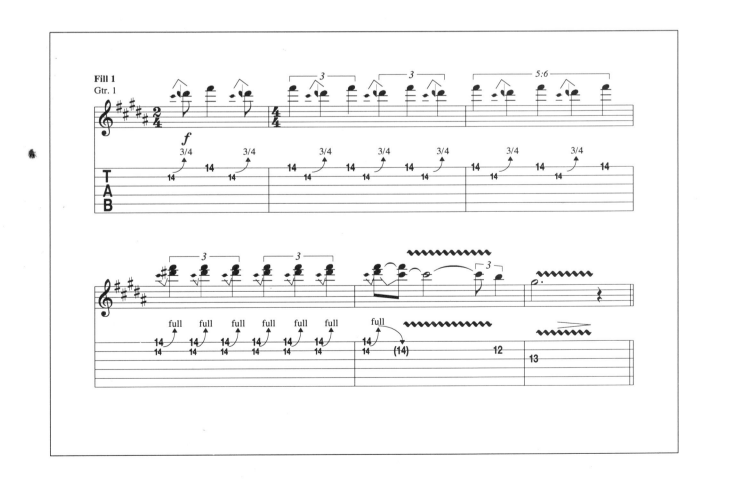

Fill 1
Gtr. 1

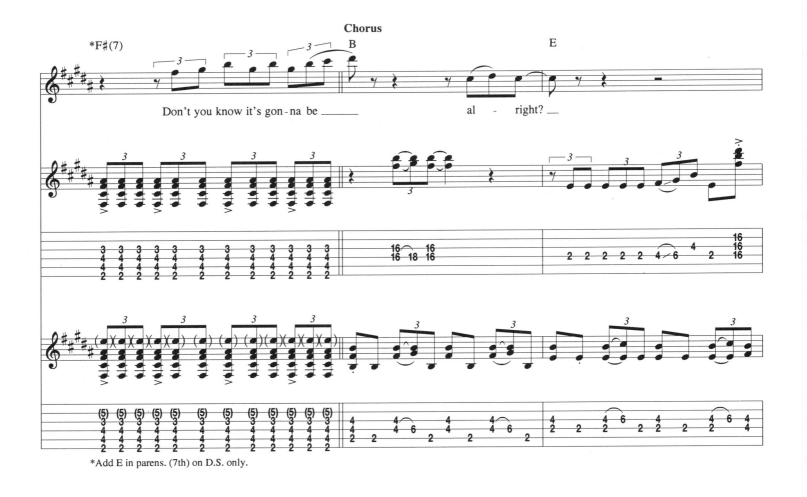

*Add E in parens. (7th) on D.S. only.

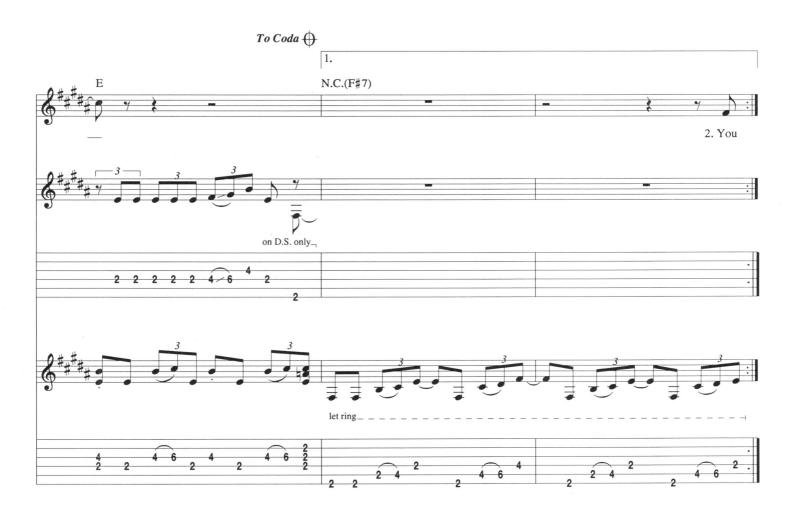

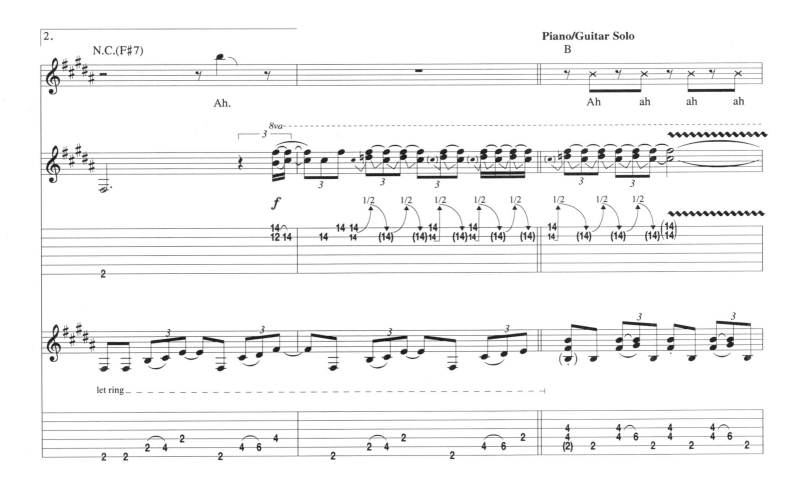

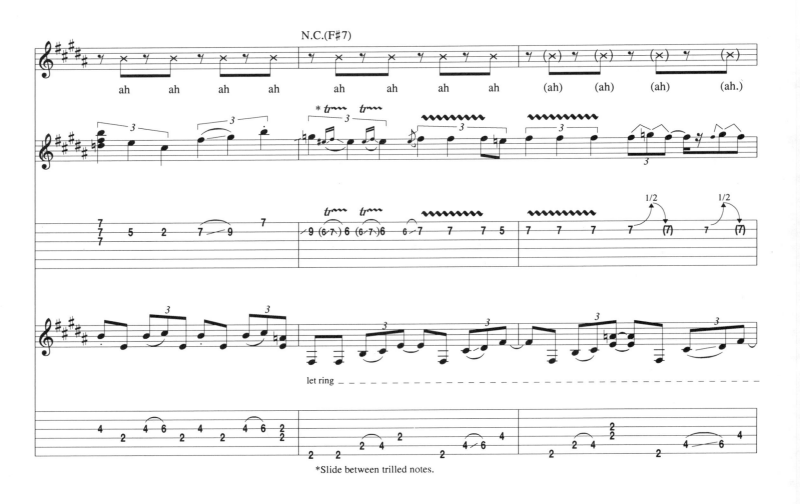

*Slide between trilled notes.

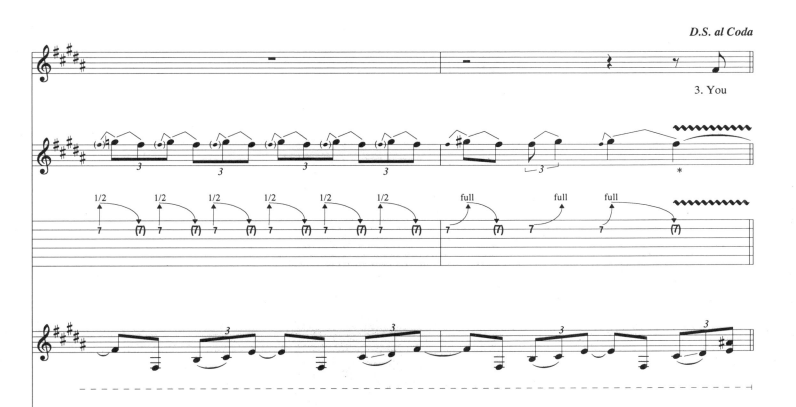

3. You

*Hold into next measure.

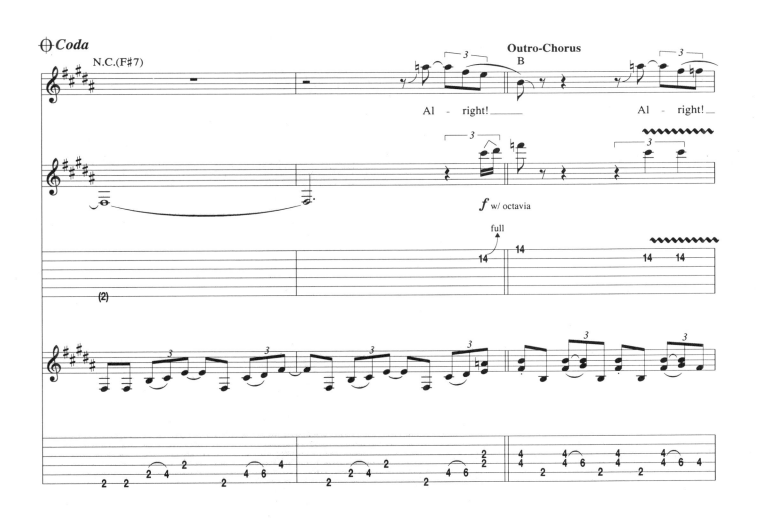

Al – right! _____   Al – right! _____   Al – right! _____

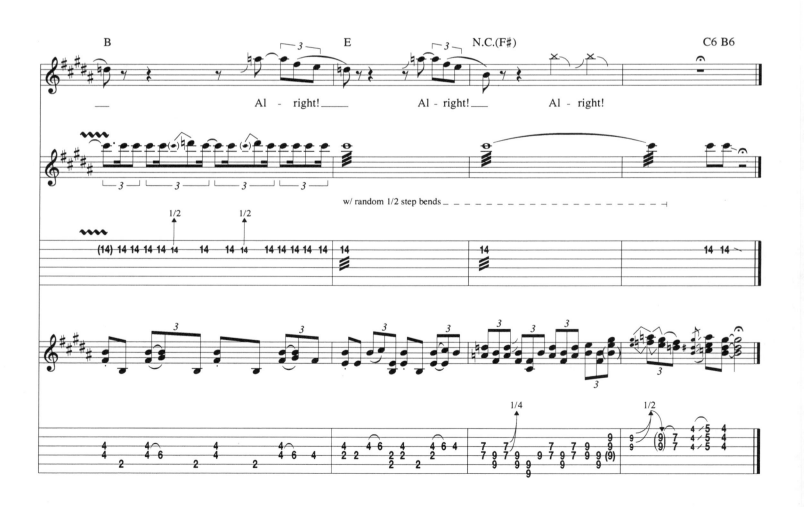

Al – right! _____   Al – right! _____   Al – right!

w/ random 1/2 step bends _ _ _ _ _ _ _ _ _ _ _ _ _ _ _ _

Back In The U.S.S.R.

Words and Music by John Lennon and Paul McCartney

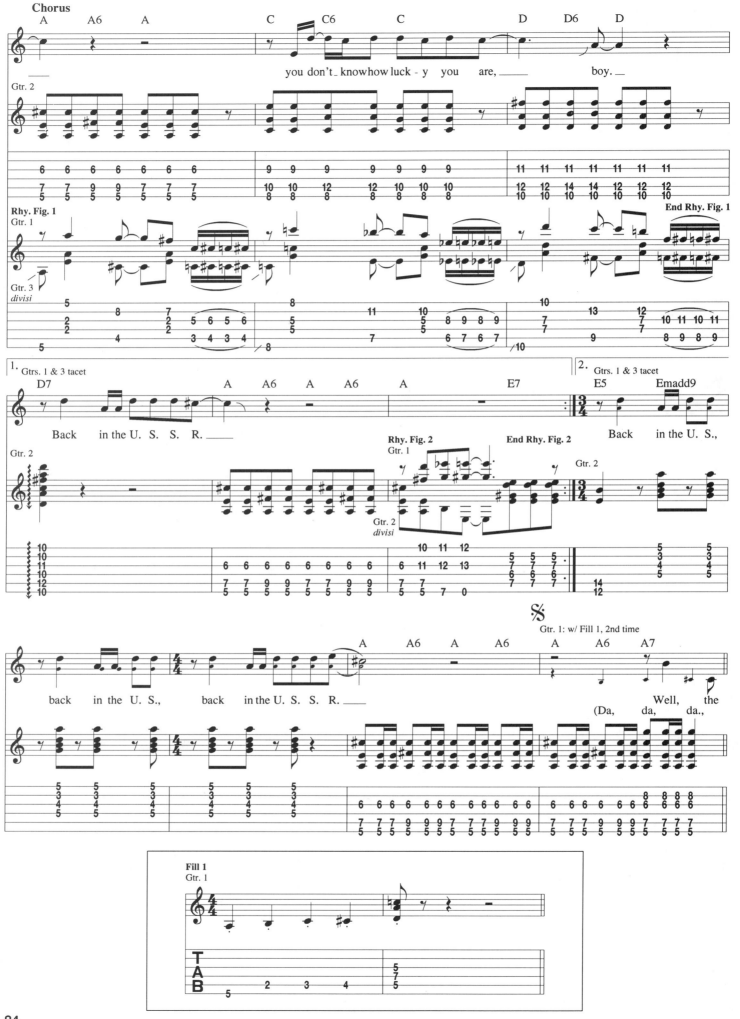

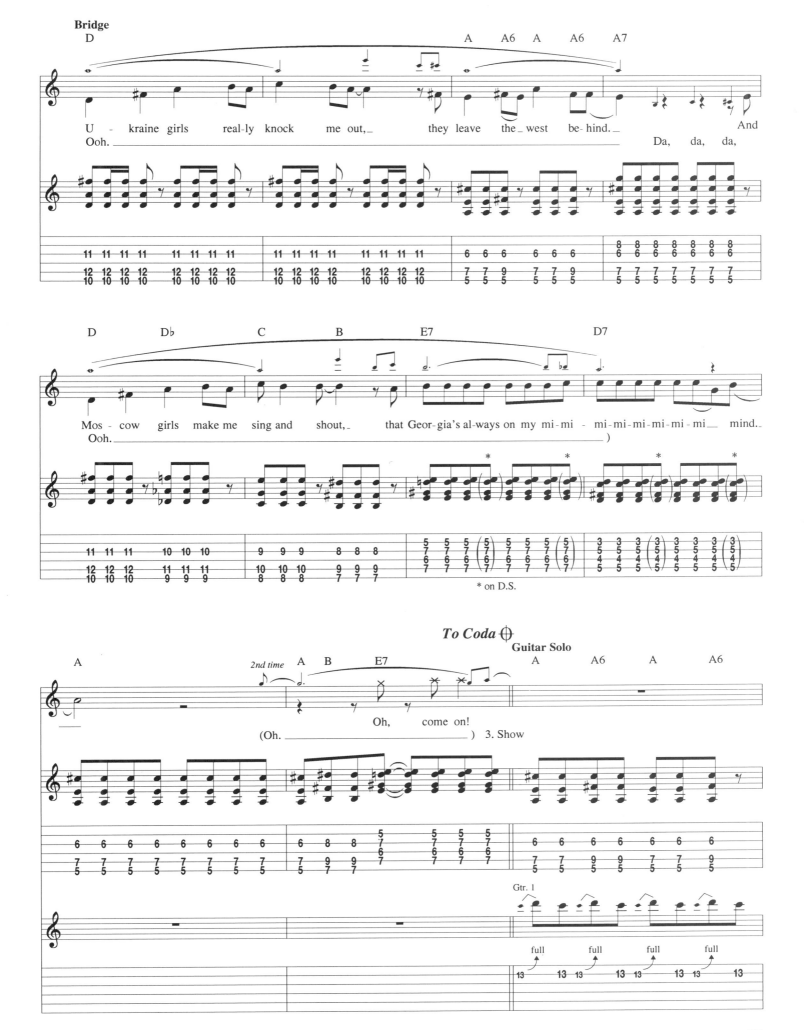

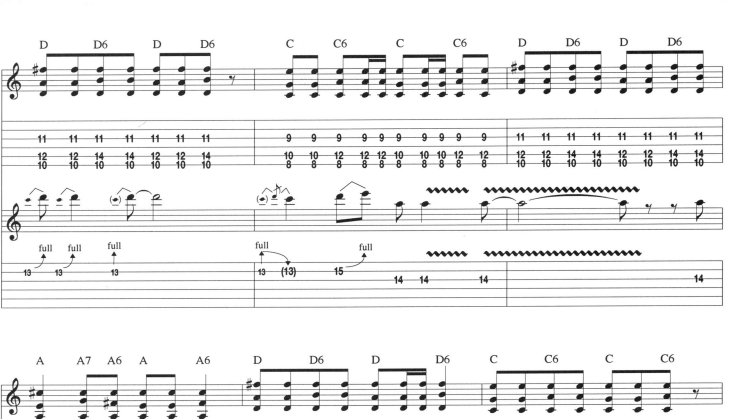

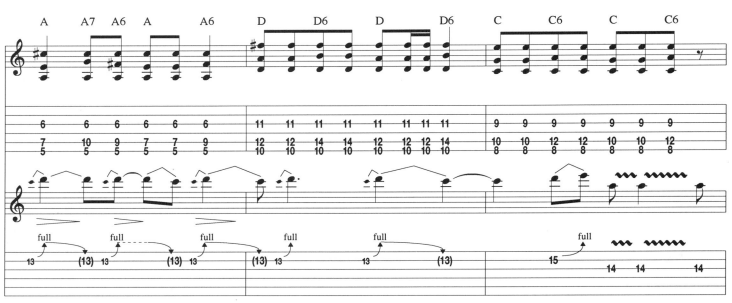

Chorus
Gtrs. 1 & 3: w/ Rhy. Fig. 1

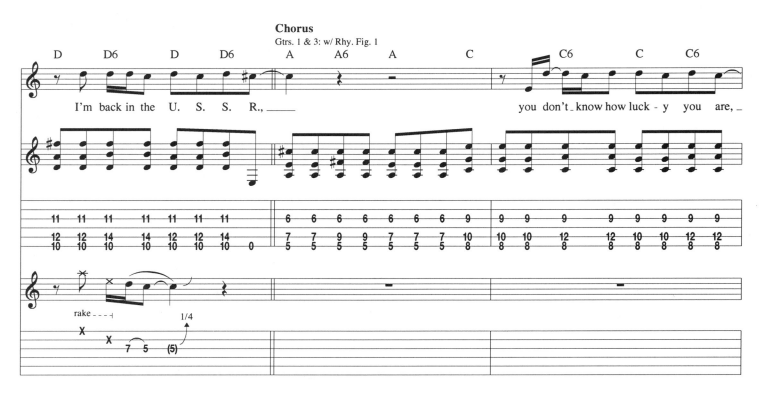

I'm back in the U. S. S. R., _____   you don't know how luck - y   you are, ___

rake

While My Guitar Gently Weeps

By George Harrison

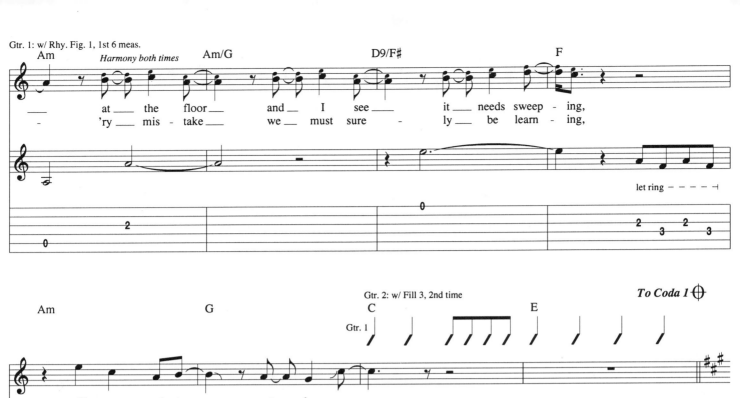

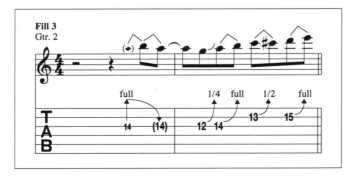

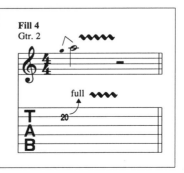

Ob - La - Di, Ob - La - Da

Words and Music by John Lennon and Paul McCartney

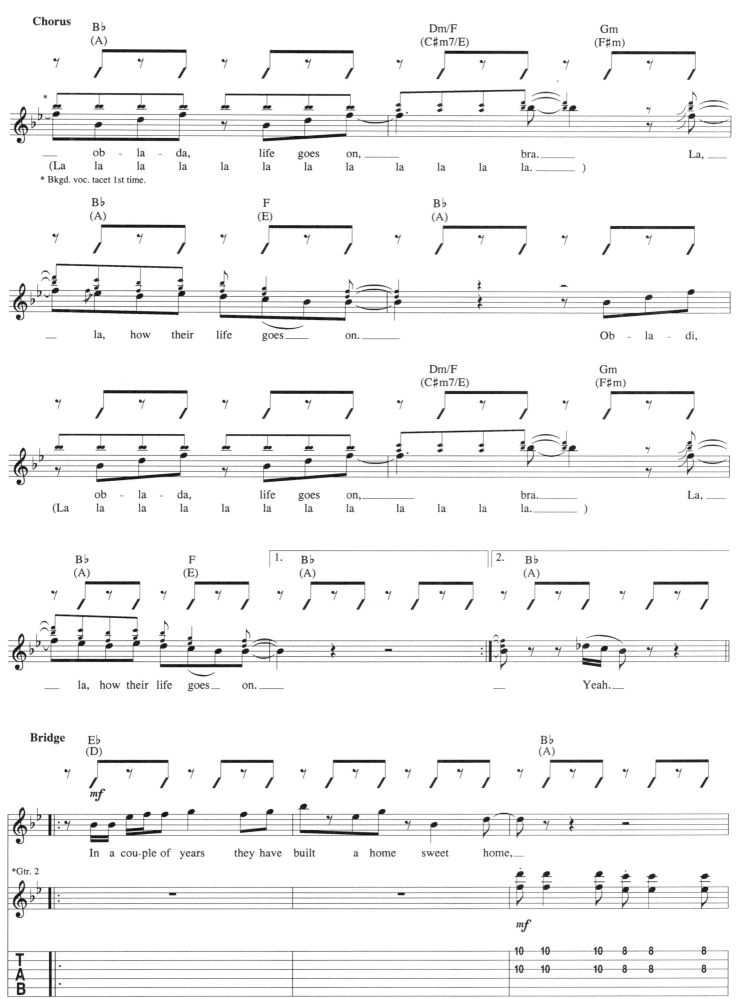

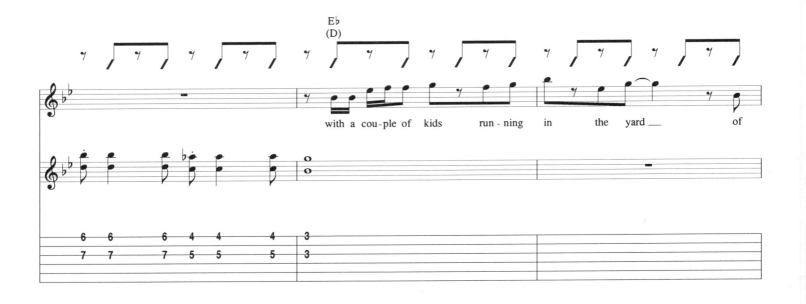

* Bkgd. voc. tacet 1st time.

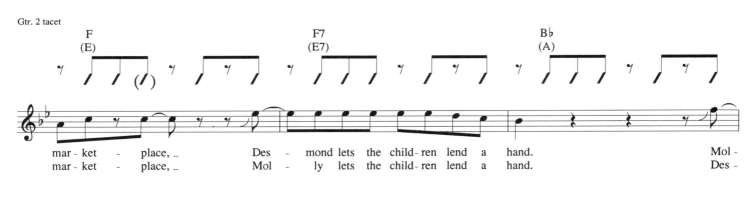

96

Yes, — } ob - la - di, ob - la - da, life goes on, ___ bra. ___ La, ___ la, how their life goes ___ on.
Yeah, — }

* Bkgd. voc. tacet 1st time.

Hey, — ob - la - di, ob - la - da, life goes on, ___ bra. ___ La, ___ la, how their life goes ___ on.

* Bkgd. voc. tacet 1st time.

Well, if you want some fun, ___ take ob - la - di - bla - da. (Thank you.)

Get Back

Words and Music by John Lennon and Paul McCartney

Intro

Moderate Rock ♩ = 123

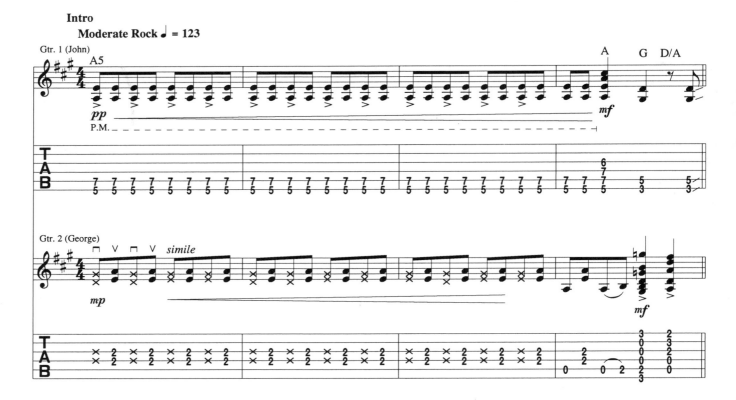

Verse

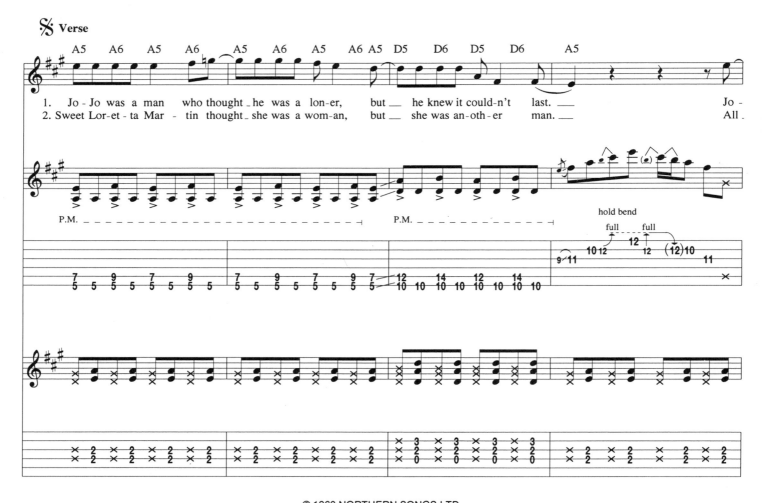

1. Jo - Jo was a man who thought _ he was a lon-er, but _ he knew it could-n't last. _ Jo -
2. Sweet Lor-et - ta Mar - tin thought _ she was a wom-an, but _ she was an-oth - er man. _ All _

Gtr. 1: w/ Fill 1, 2nd time

- Jo left his home in Tu - scon, A - ri - zo - na for _ some Ca - li - for - nia grass. _
- the girls a - round her say _ she's got it com - ing but she gets it while she can. _

Get back,_

Chorus

*A7#9   N.C. (A6)   A7#9   N.C. (D)   D7   N.C. (A6)   G   D/A

_ get back,_   get back _ to where you once be - longed. _

Get back,_

* Chord symbols reflect overall harmony.

Fill 1
Gtr. 1

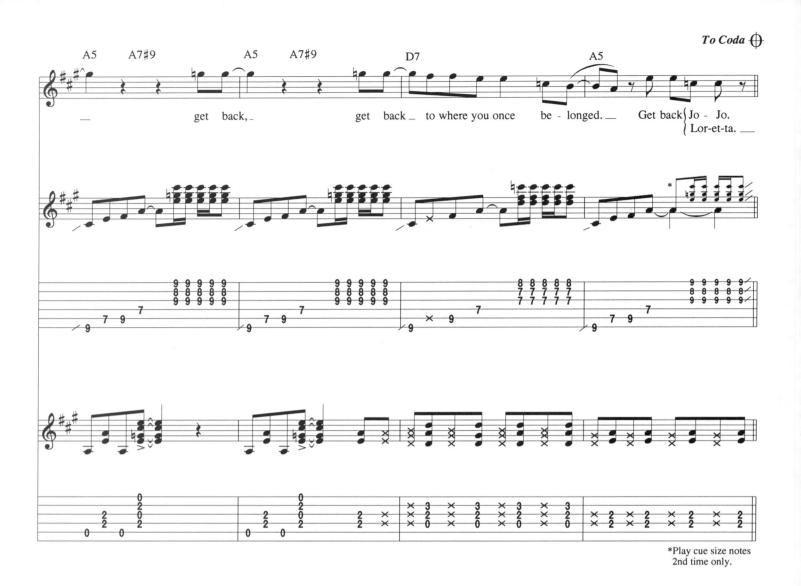

get back, ___ get back ___ to where you once be - longed. ___ Get back { Jo - Jo.
{ Lor-et-ta. ___

*Play cue size notes
2nd time only.

Guitar Solo

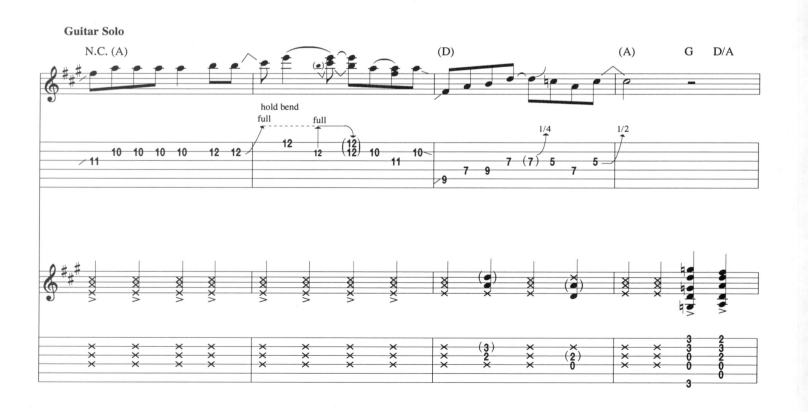

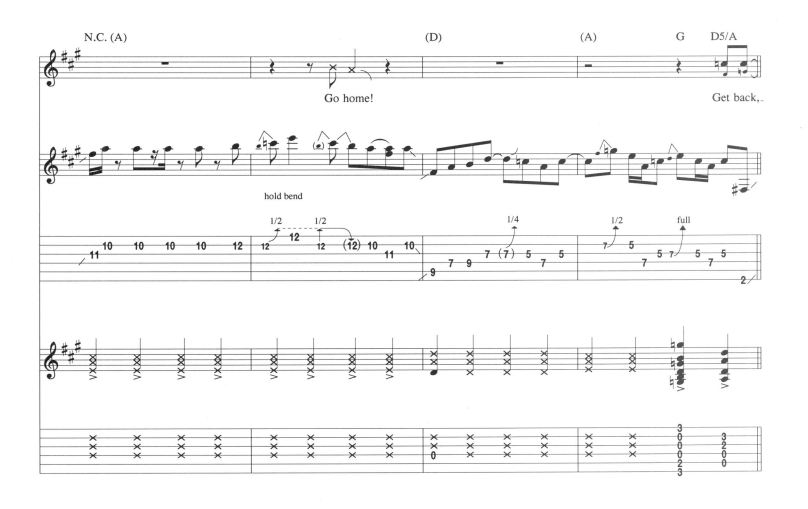

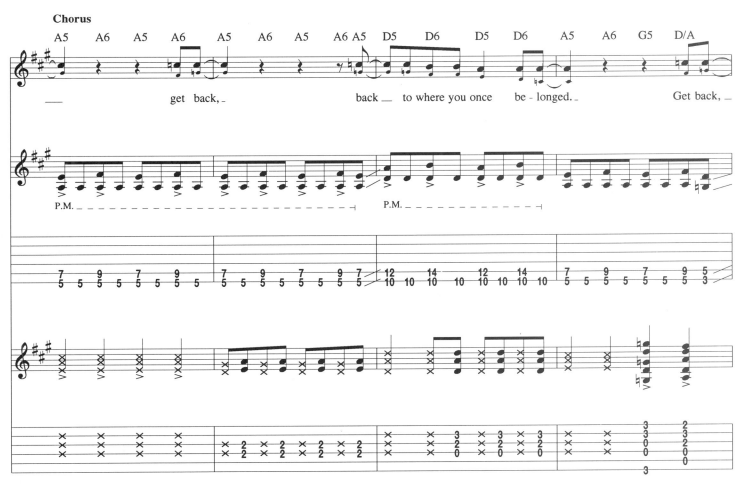

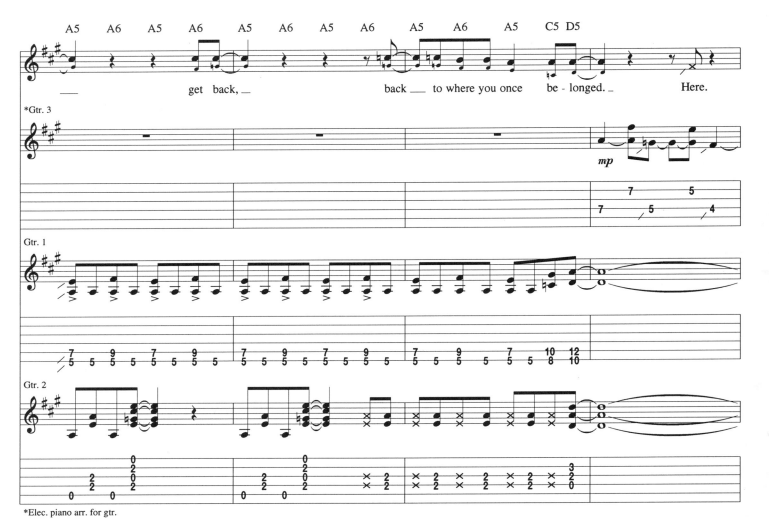

get back, ___ back ___ to where you once be - longed. ___ Here.

*Gtr. 3

mp

Gtr. 1

Gtr. 2

*Elec. piano arr. for gtr.

Uh, get back Jo!

Piano Solo

8va - - - - - - - - - - - - - -

 Coda

Guitar Solo

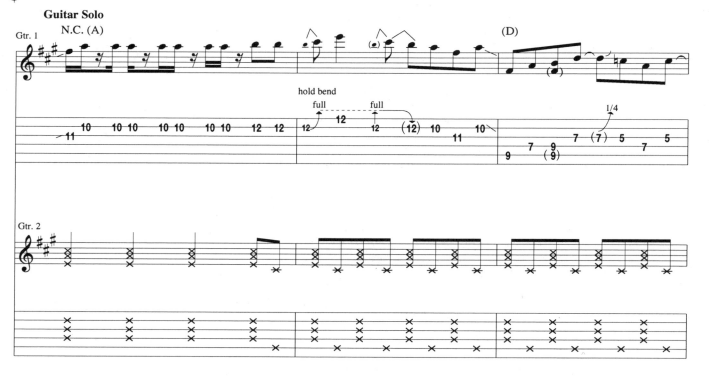

104

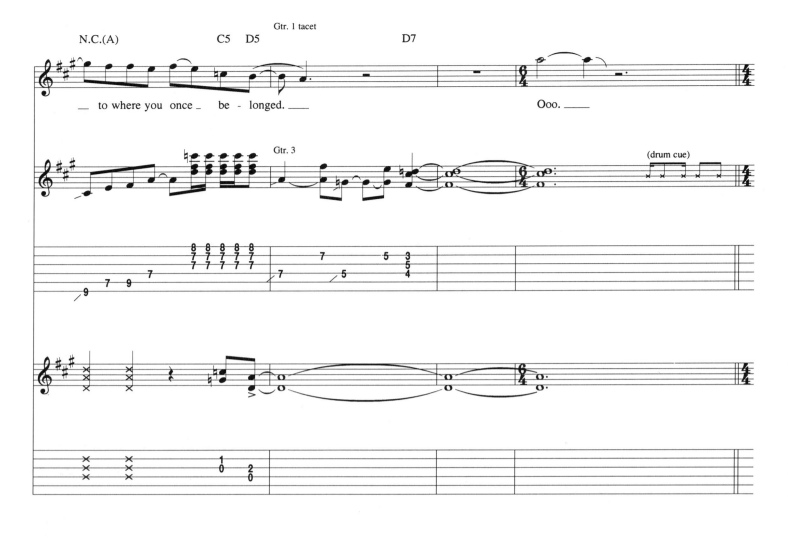

Outro
Gtr. 3 tacet

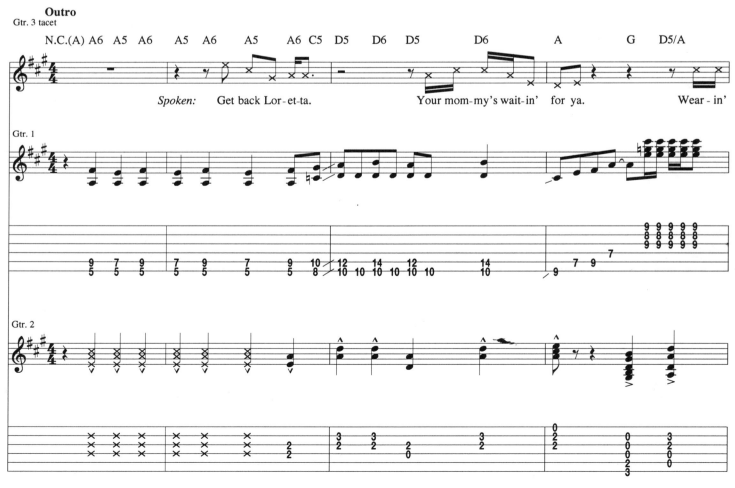

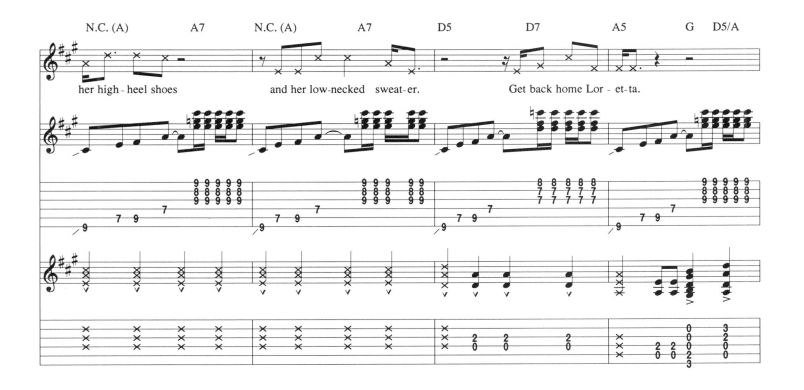

her high - heel shoes   and her low-necked sweat-er.   Get back home Lor - et-ta.

Lead voc. ad lib till fade

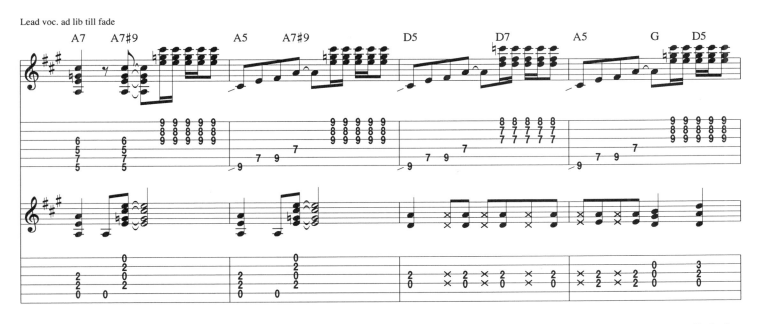

Begin Fade

Fade Out

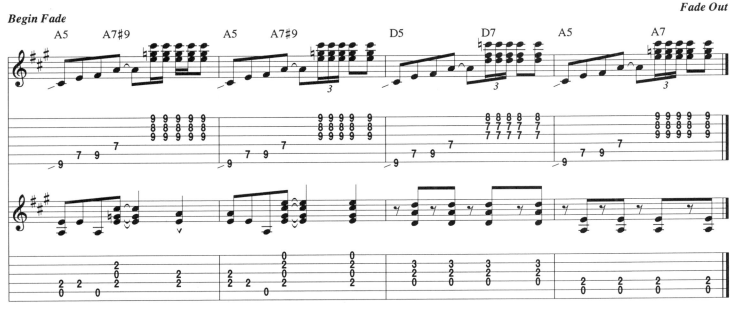

Don't Let Me Down

Words and Music by John Lennon and Paul McCartney

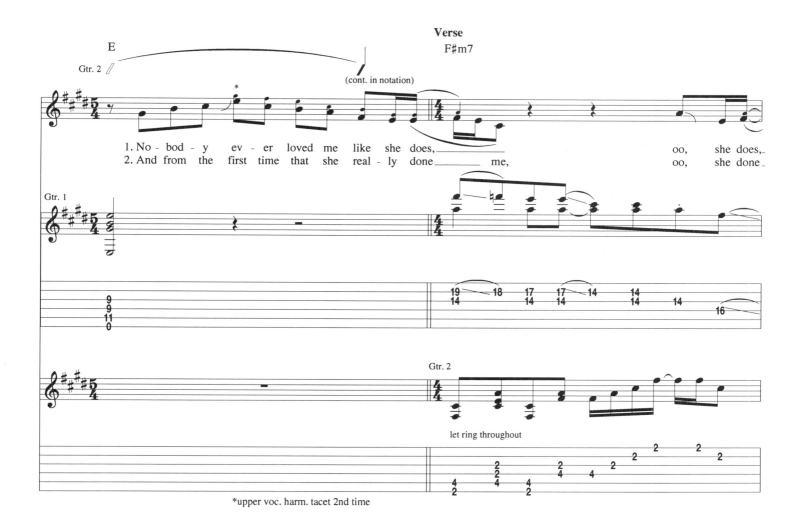

Verse

1. No-bod-y ev-er loved me like she does, oo, she does,
2. And from the first time that she real-ly done me, oo, she done

*upper voc. harm. tacet 2nd time

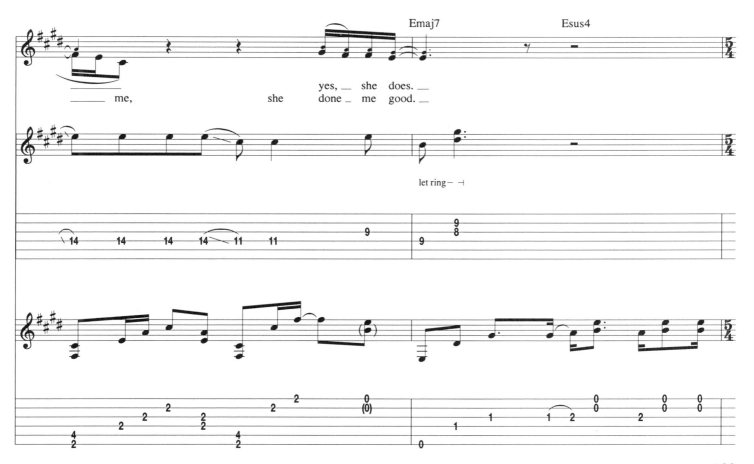

me, she done me good.

yes, she does.

And if some-bod-y loved me like she do _____ me,   oo, she do __
I guess no-bod-y ev-er real-ly done me,   oo, she done __

*upper voc. harm. barely audible 2nd time

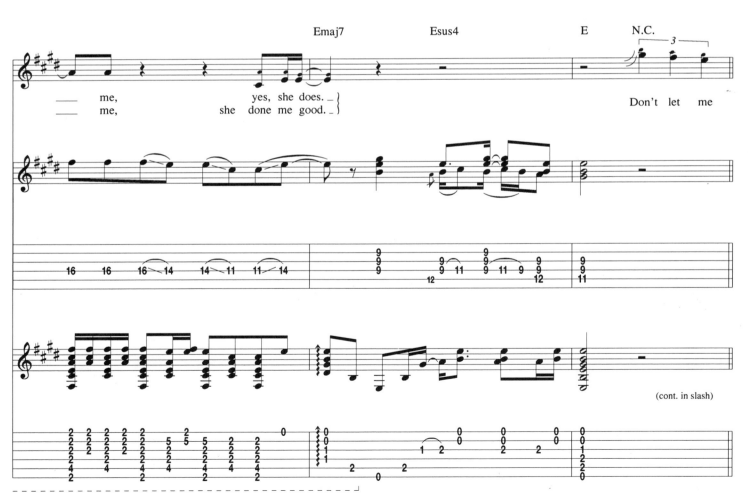

__ me,   yes, she does. __ }
__ me,   she done me good. __ }

Don't let me

(cont. in slash)

The Ballad Of John And Yoko

Words and Music by John Lennon and Paul McCartney

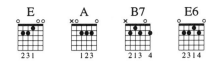

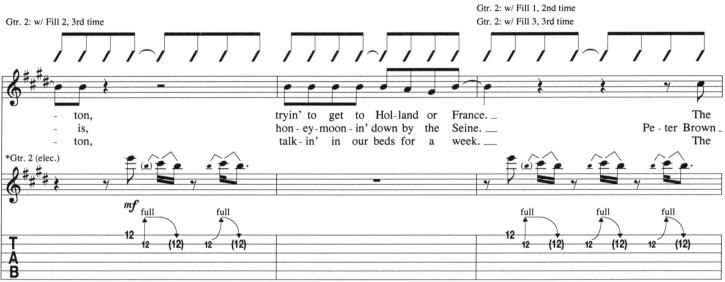

*Two gtrs. arr. for one.

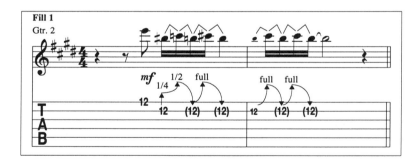

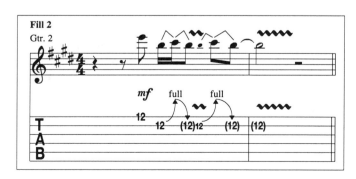

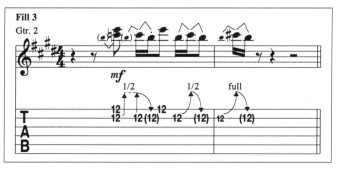

man in the mac ___ said, "You've got - ta go back." You know they did - n't e - ven give us a chance. ___
___ called to say, ___ "You can make it O. K., you can get mar - ried in Gib - ral - tar near Spain."
news - peo - ple said, ___ "Say, what - cha do - in' in bed?" I said, "We're on - ly tryin' to get us some peace."

Chorus
A

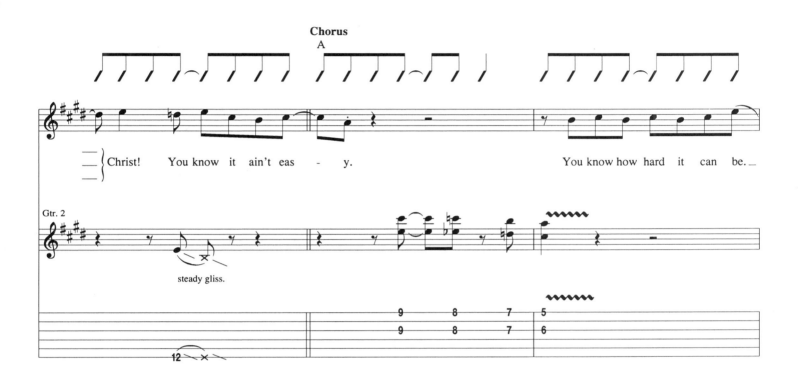

___ { Christ! You know it ain't eas - y.   You know how hard it can be. ___

Gtr. 2

steady gliss.

E   B7

The way things are go - in' ___

they're gon - na cru - ci - fy ___ me.

3. Drove from

Sav - in' up your mon - ey for a

steady gliss.   P.M. throughout

rain - y day, ___   giv-in' all   your clothes to char - i - ty.

Last night the wife said, "Oh boy, when you're dead you don't take noth-in' with you but your

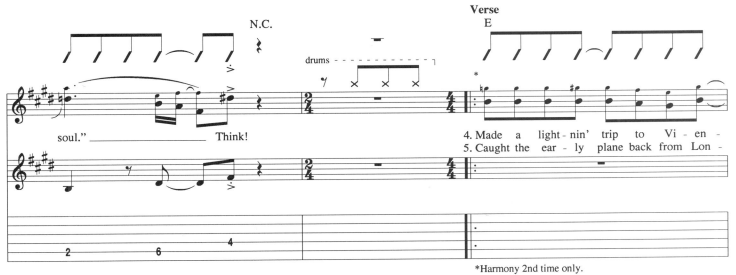

soul." _____ Think!

Harmony 2nd time only.

Verse

4. Made a light-nin' trip to Vi - en -
5. Caught the ear - ly plane back from Lon -

Gtr. 2: w/ Fill 4, 2nd time

Gtr. 2: w/ Fill 5, 2nd time

- na,
- don,

eat - ing choc'-late cake in a bag. _____
fif - ty a - corns tied in a sack. _____

The
The

Fill 4
Gtr. 3

Gtr. 2
divisi

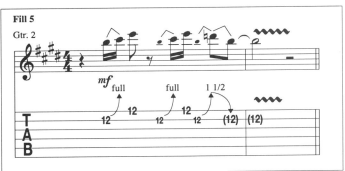

Fill 5
Gtr. 2

Gtr. 2: w/ Fill 6, 2nd time

news - pa - per said, ___ "She's gone to his head. ___ They look just like two Gu - rus in drag."
men from the press ___ said, "We wish you suc - cess. ___ It's good to have the both of you back."

full

Chorus

A

Christ! You know it ain't eas - y. You know how hard it can be. ___

steady gliss.

E

B7

The way things are go - in' ___

Fill 6

Gtr. 2

mf

they're gon - na cru - ci - fy ____ me.

* Gtr. 2 indicated to right of slash.

me.   The way things are   go   -   in' ____

they're gon - na   cru - ci - fy ____   me.

Outro

Old Brown Shoe

Words and Music by George Harrison

* piano and bass arr. for gtr.

*Chord symbols reflect overall harmony.

Interlude

Guitar Solo

123

Here Comes The Sun

Words and Music by George Harrison

*Capo VII

Intro
Moderately ♩ = 126

Gtr. 1 (acous.)

mf let ring throughout

*All notes tabbed on 7th fret are played as open strings

Chorus

Here comes _ the sun,____ doo 'n' doo doo. Here comes _ the sun _

_ 'n' I ___ say _ it's al - right.

Lit - tle dar-lin', it ___ seems ___ like ___ years ___ since it's ___ been ___ clear. ___

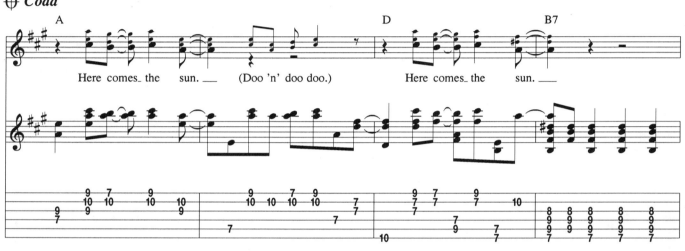

⊕ *Coda*

Here comes ___ the sun. ___ (Doo 'n' doo doo.) Here comes ___ the sun. ___

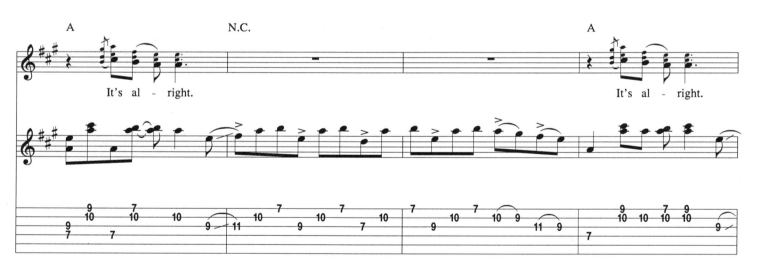

It's al - right. It's al - right.

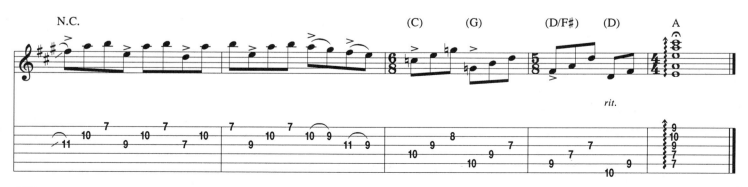

rit.

Come Together

Words and Music by John Lennon and Paul McCartney

Intro
Moderately Slow Rock ♩ = 84

Verse

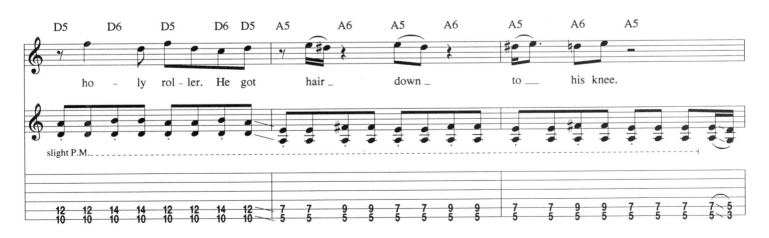

Guitar Solo

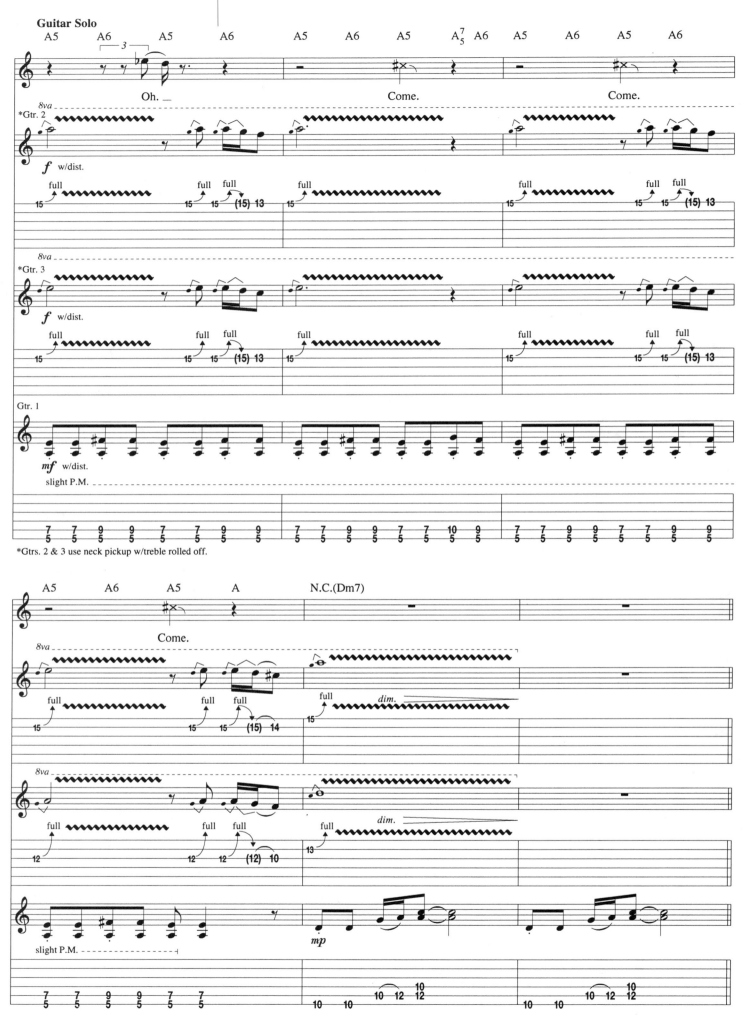

*Gtrs. 2 & 3 use neck pickup w/treble rolled off.

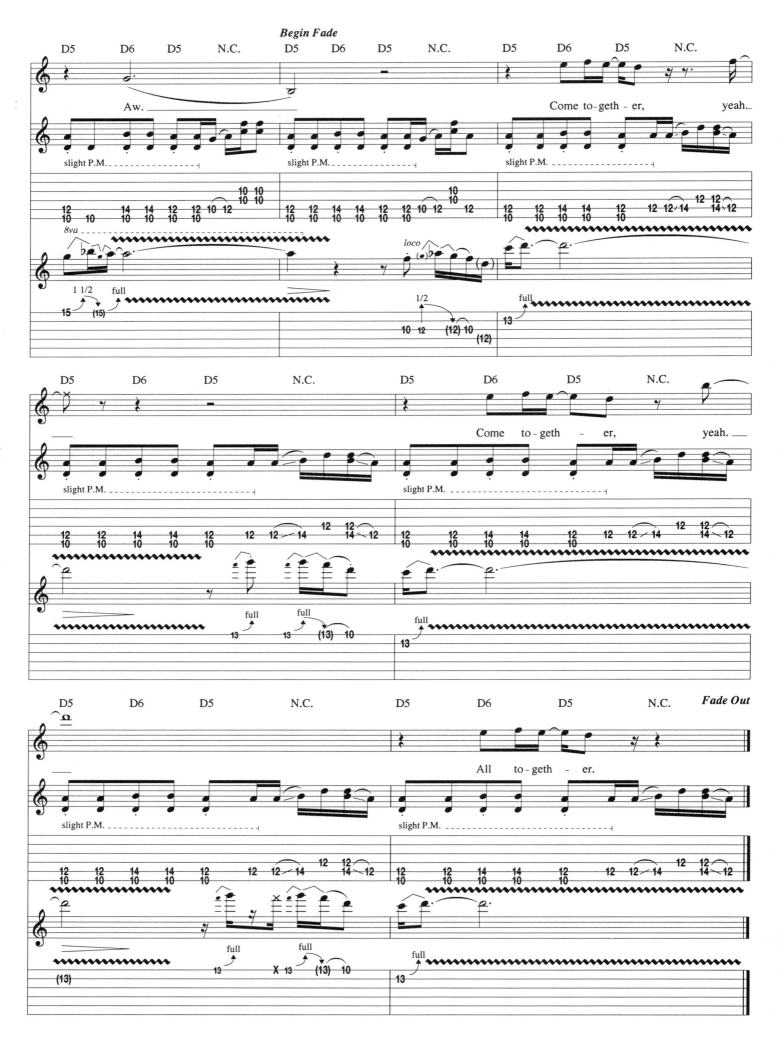

Verse
Gtrs. 2 & 3 tacet
D5 D6 D5 N.C. D5 D6 D5 N.C. D5 D6 D5 N.C.
4. He rol - ler coast - er, he got ear - ly warn-ing. He got mud - dy wa - ter, he one
Gtr. 1
mf
slight P.M.
let ring
D7 D5 D6 D5 N.C. A5 A6 A5 N.C. A5 A6 A5 N.C.
Mo - jo fil - ter. He say, "One and one and one is three."
G5 N.C. B5 B5/A
Got to be good look - in' 'cause he's so hard to see. Come to - geth - er, right
f
G5 A5 N.C. (Dm7)
now, ov - er me.
Whispered: Shoot me.
mp
Gtr. 2
w/vol. pedal

Something

Words and Music by George Harrison

Gtr. 3; "Drop D" Tuning:

① = E   ④ = D
② = B   ⑤ = A
③ = G   ⑥ = D

Gtrs. 1 & 2: Standard Tuning

Intro

Slowly ♩ = 66

(drums)

1. Some-thing in ___ the way   she moves ___
2. Some-where in ___ her smile   she knows ___

Gtr. 1

mf
w/clean tone

Gtr. 2

mf
w/ Leslie

simile, 2nd time

Gtr. 1 tacet

at-tracts ___ me like   no   oth-er   lov-
that I ___ don't need   no   oth-er   lov-

Gtr. 2

let ⑤ ring ___

- er.
- er.

Some-thing in ___ the way   she ___ woos ___
Some-thing in ___ the style   that ___ shows ___

let ring

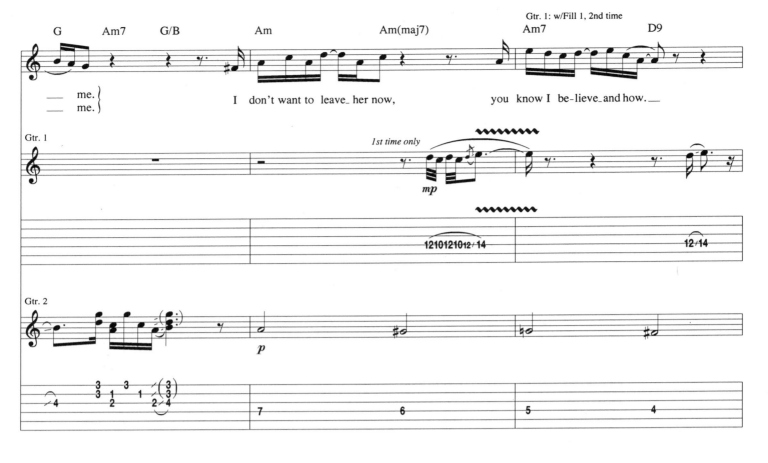

I don't want to leave her now, you know I believe and how.

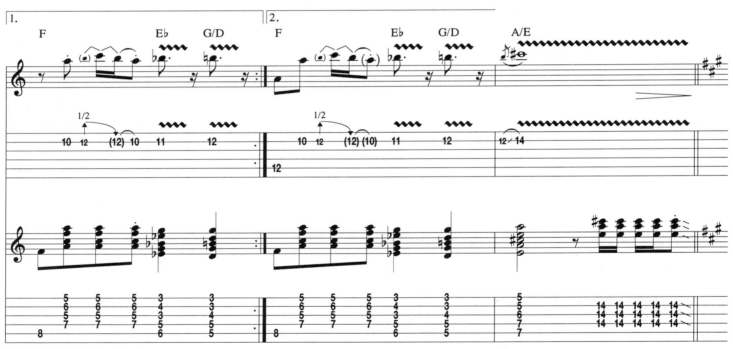

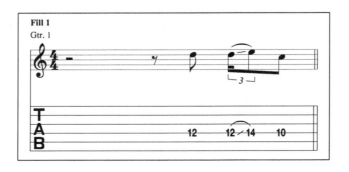

Fill 1

Gtr. 1

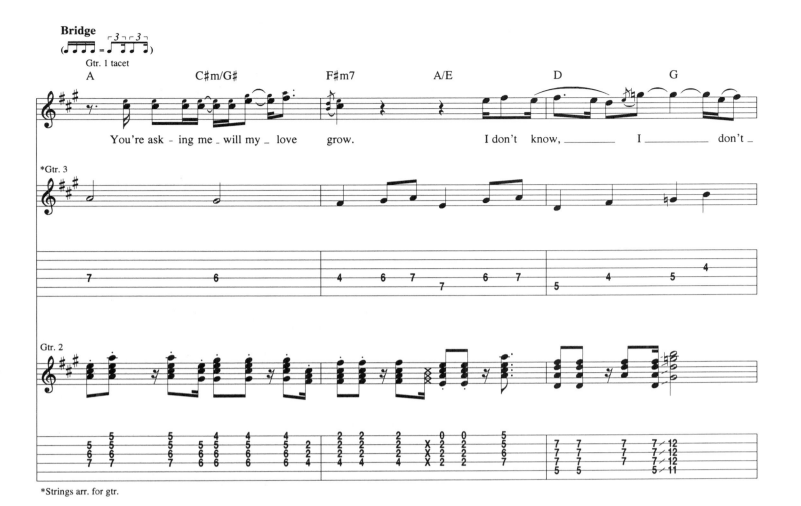

*Strings arr. for gtr.

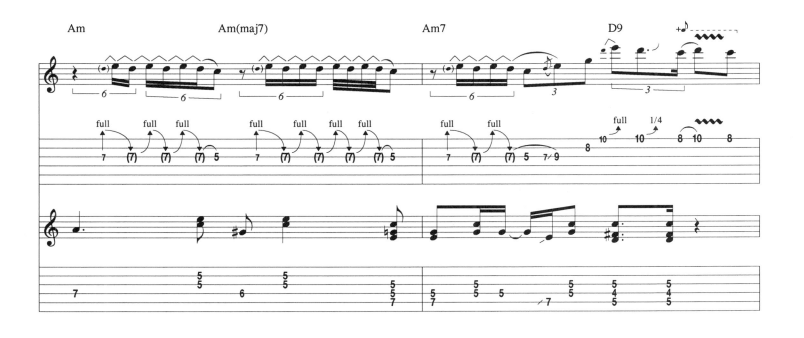

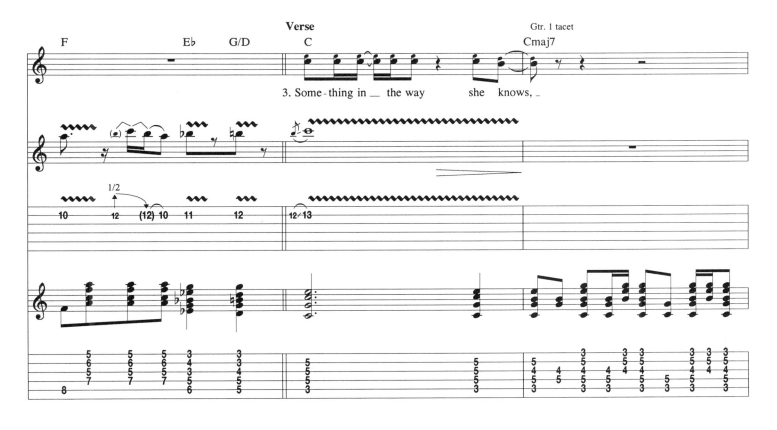

Verse

Gtr. 1 tacet

3. Some-thing in __ the way she knows, __

and all __ I have _____ to do _____ is think of her.

Gtr. 2

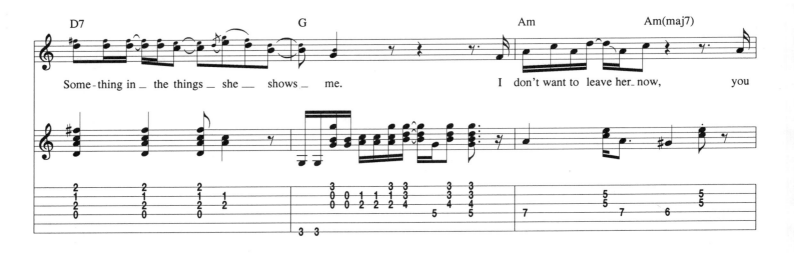

Some-thing in _ the things _ she _ shows _ me.   I don't want to leave her _ now,   you

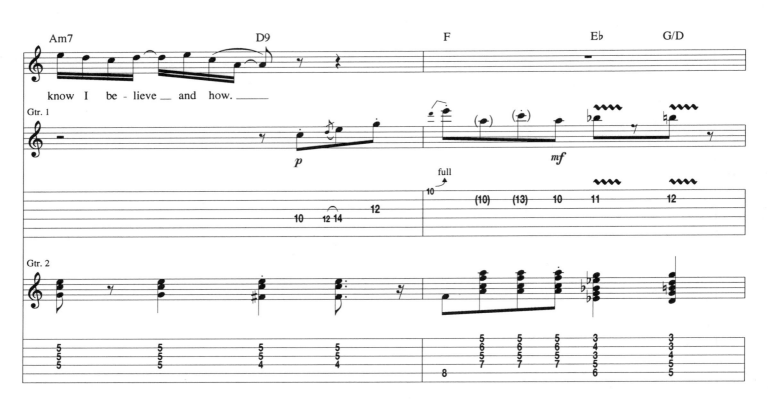

know I be - lieve _ and how. _____

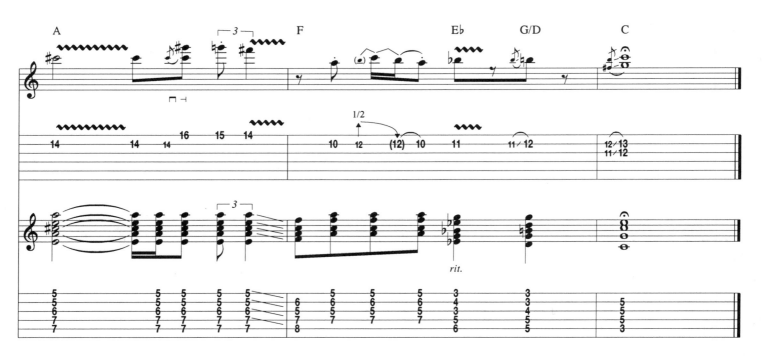

Octopus's Garden

Words and Music by Richard Starkey

Verse

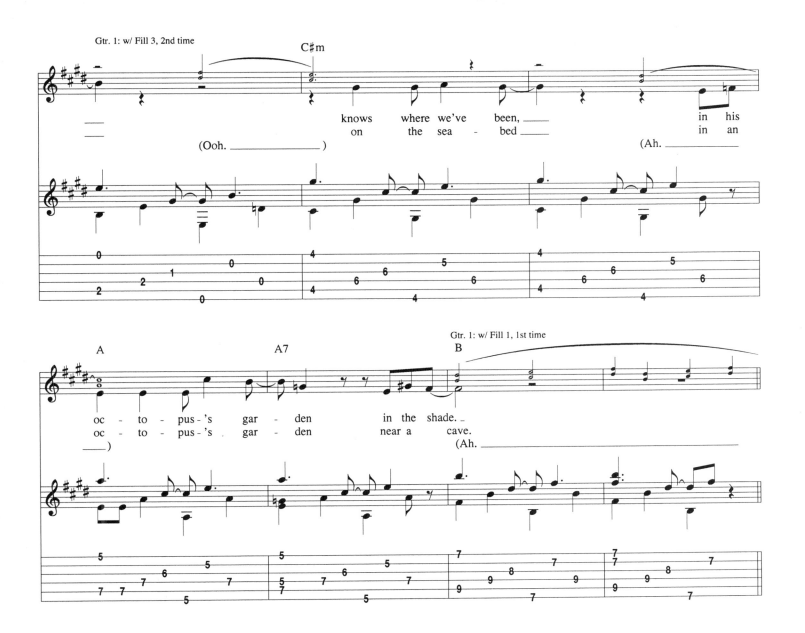

knows where we've been, _____ in his

on the sea - bed _____ in an

(Ooh. _____) (Ah. _____

oc - to - pus - 's gar - den in the shade. _____

oc - to - pus - 's gar - den near a cave.

_____) (Ah. _____

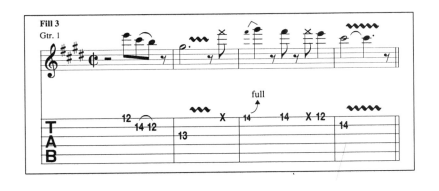

Fill 3
Gtr. 1

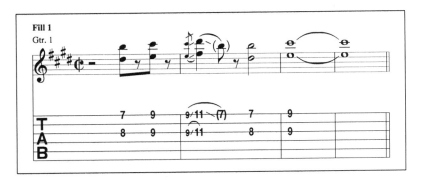

Fill 1
Gtr. 1

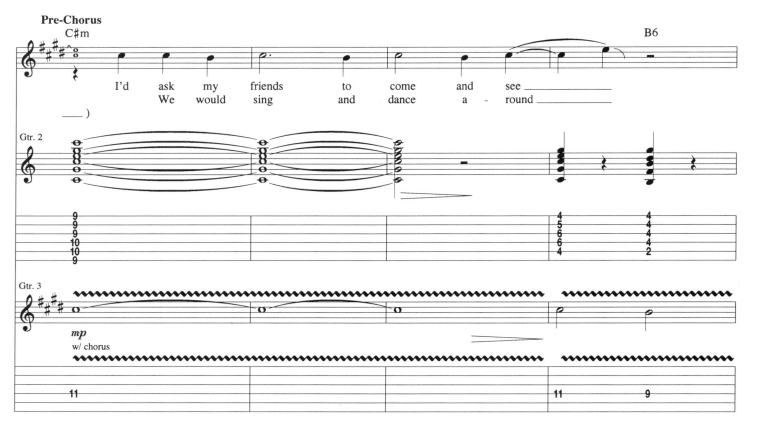

I'd ask my friends to come and see _____
We would sing and dance a - round _____

_____)

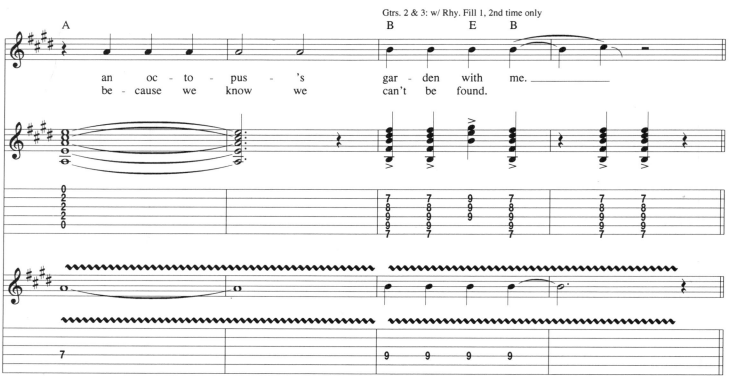

an oc - to - pus - 's gar - den with me. _____
be - cause we know we can't be found.

Gtrs. 2 & 3: w/ Rhy. Fill 1, 2nd time only

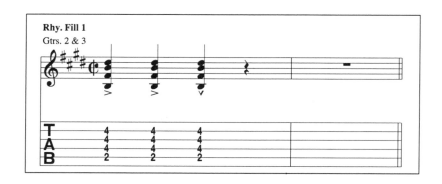

Rhy. Fill 1
Gtrs. 2 & 3

I'd like to be _____ un - der the sea _____ in an

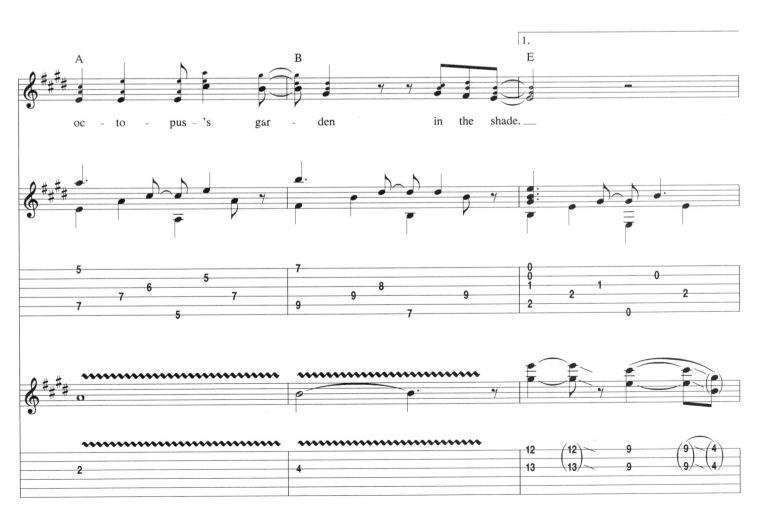

oc - to - pus - 's gar - den in the shade. _____

Guitar Solo

Verse
Gtr. 1 tacet

3. We would shout ___ and ___ swim a - bout ___
(Ah. ___)

Gtr. 2

___ the cor - al ___ that lies ___ be - neath the waves. ___
(Ooh. ___)

(Lies be - neath the o - cean waves.)
Oh, what joy ___

for ev - 'ry girl and boy, ___
(Ah. ___)
(Ooh. ___)

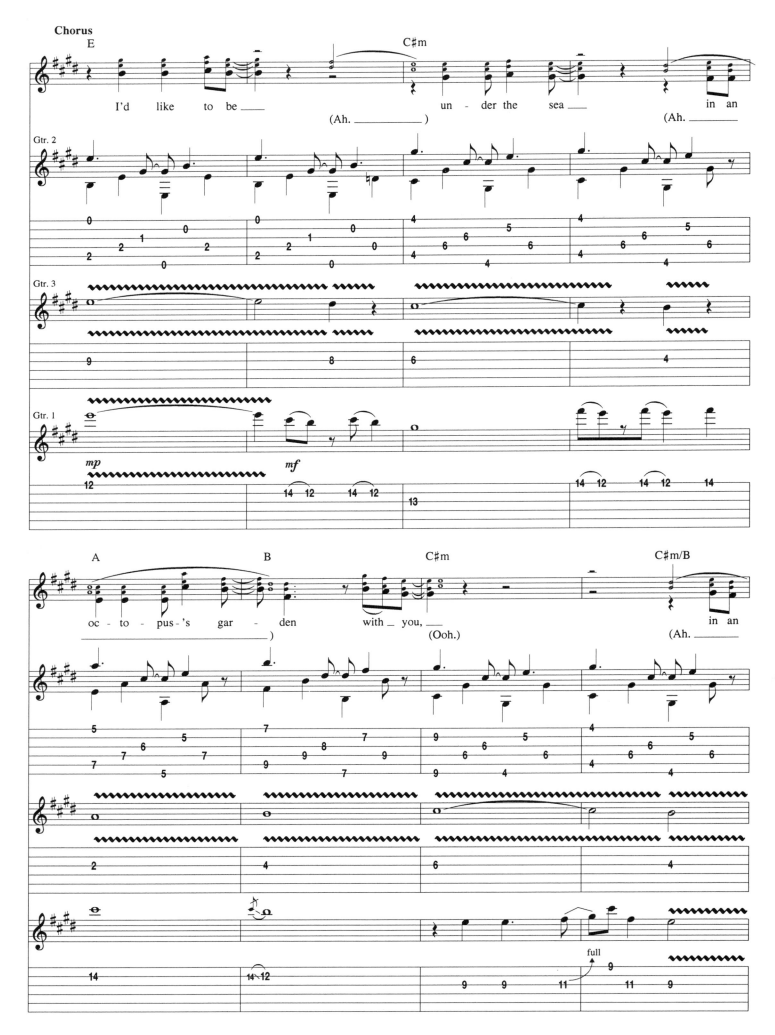

Let It Be

Words and Music by John Lennon and Paul McCartney

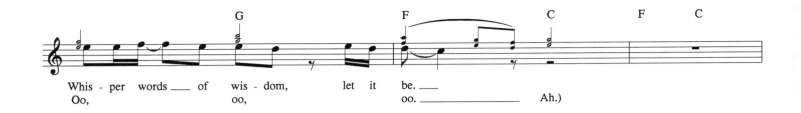

Whis - per words ___ of wis - dom,   let it be. ___
Oo,   oo,   oo. ___ Ah.)

D.S. al Coda

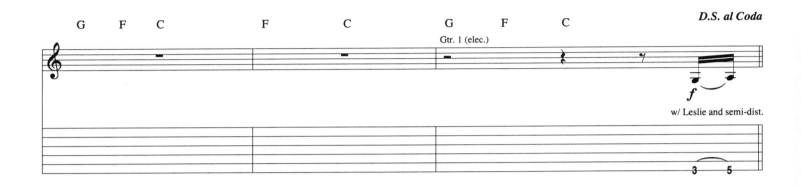

Gtr. 1 (elec.)

f

w/ Leslie and semi-dist.

⊕ *Coda*

be, ___ hee, ah. Let it be, ___ let it be.   Ah, let it be, ___ yeah, let it be. ___
oo,   oo.   Oo,   oo,   oo,   oo.)

Gtr. 1

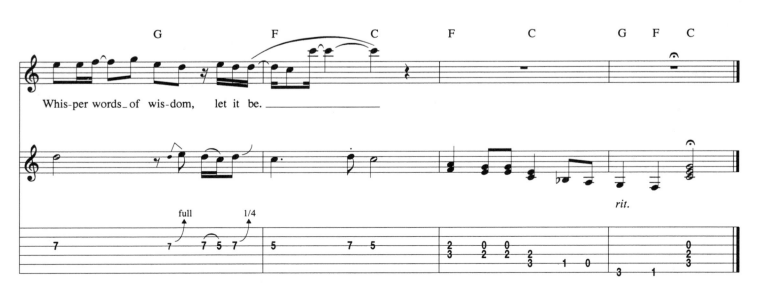

Whis - per words _ of wis - dom,   let it be. ___

rit.

Across The Universe

Words and Music by John Lennon and Paul McCartney

Noth-ing's gon-na change my world. ___

Noth-ing's gon-na change my world. ___ Noth-ing's gon-na change my world. ___

To Coda ⊕ **Verse**

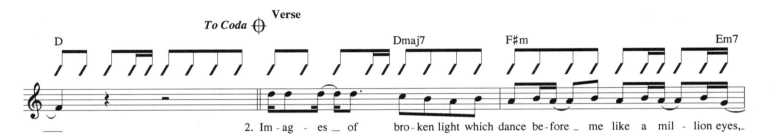

2. Im - ag - es ___ of bro-ken light which dance be-fore ___ me like a mil - lion eyes,

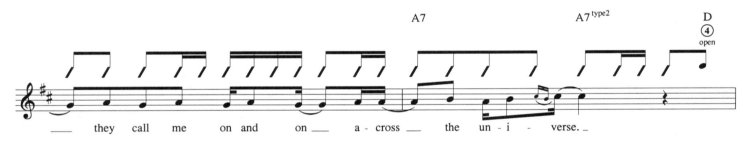

___ they call me on and on ___ a - cross ___ the un - i - verse.

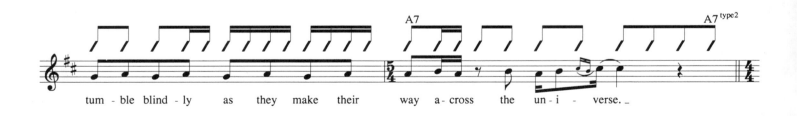

Thoughts me - an - der like a rest - less wind in - side a let - ter box, ___ they

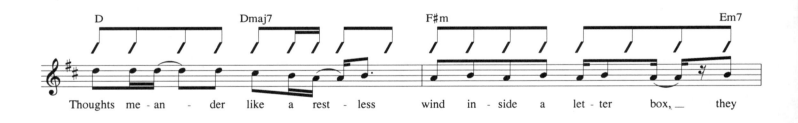

tum - ble blind - ly as they make their way a - cross the un - i - verse. ___

Chorus

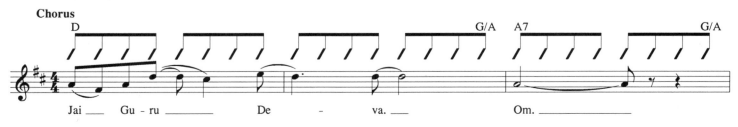

Jai ___ Gu - ru ___ De - va. ___ Om. ___

The Long And Winding Road

Words and Music by John Lennon and Paul McCartney

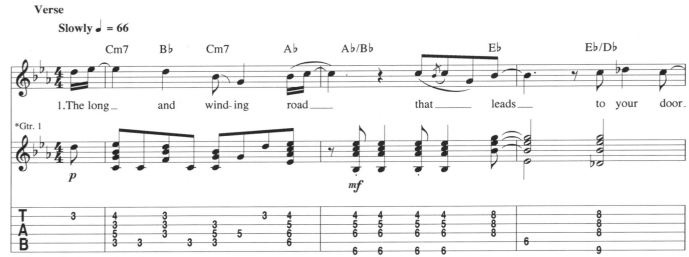

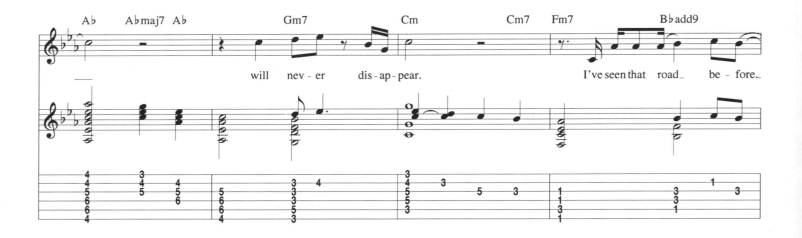

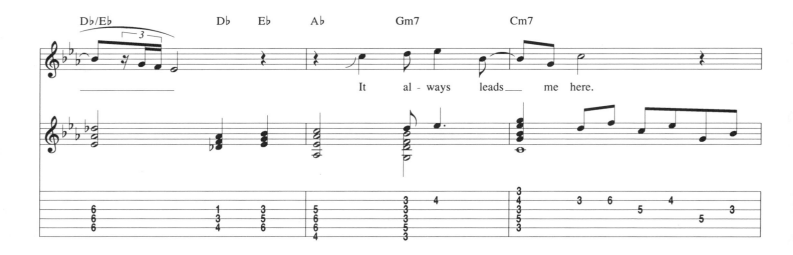

Lead me to your door.

2. The wild and wind-y night
3., 4. still they lead me back

*Parenthesized notes are strings arr. for gtr.
Play high G second time and full chord on D.S.

Gtr. 2: w/ Fill 1, 1st time

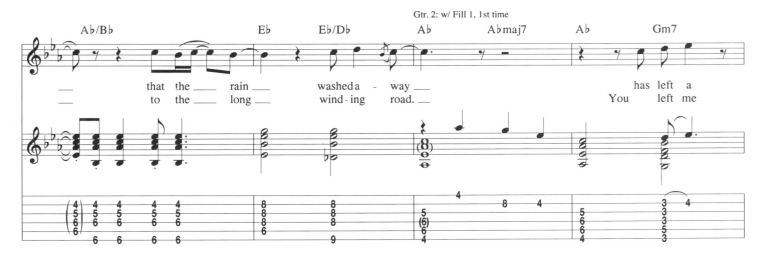

that the rain washed a - way
to the long wind-ing road. You left me
has left a

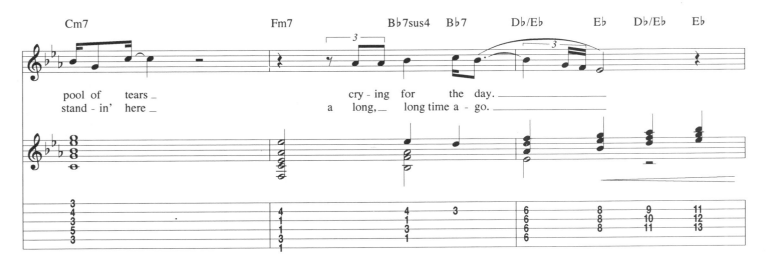

pool of tears
stand-in' here
cry-ing for the day.
a long, long time a - go.

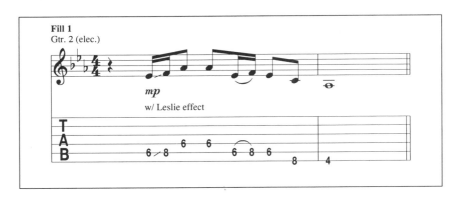

Fill 1
Gtr. 2 (elec.)

mp

w/ Leslie effect

NOTATION LEGEND

RECORDED VERSIONS
The Best Note-For-Note Transcriptions Available

RECORDED VERSIONS GUITAR

ALL BOOKS INCLUDE TABLATURE

00690002 Aerosmith – Big Ones	$22.95
00694909 Aerosmith – Get A Grip	$19.95
00692015 Aerosmith's Greatest Hits	$19.95
00660133 Aerosmith – Pump	$19.95
00694865 Alice In Chains – Dirt	$19.95
00660225 Alice In Chains – Facelift	$19.95
00694925 Alice In Chains – Jar Of Flies/Sap	$19.95
00694932 Allman Brothers Band – Vol. 1	$24.95
00694933 Allman Brothers Band – Vol. 2	$24.95
00694934 Allman Brothers Band – Vol. 3	$24.95
00694826 Anthrax – Attack Of The Killer B's	$19.95
00694876 Chet Atkins – Contemporary Styles	$19.95
00694918 The Randy Bachman Collection	$22.95
00660051 Badlands	$19.95
00694929 Beatles: 1962-1966	$24.95
00694930 Beatles: 1967-1970	$24.95
00694880 Beatles – Abbey Road	$19.95
00694832 Beatles For Acoustic Guitar	$19.95
00660140 Beatles Guitar Book	$19.95
00694891 Beatles – Revolver	$19.95
00694914 Beatles – Rubber Soul	$19.95
00694863 Beatles – Sgt. Pepper's Lonely Hearts Club Band	$19.95
00694931 Belly – Star	$19.95
00694884 The Best of George Benson	$19.95
00692385 Chuck Berry	$19.95
00692200 Black Sabbath – We Sold Our Soul For Rock 'N' Roll	$19.95
00694821 Blue Heaven – Great Blues Guitar	$19.95
00694770 Jon Bon Jovi – Blaze Of Glory	$19.95
00690008 Bon Jovi – Cross Road	$19.95
00694871 Bon Jovi – Keep The Faith	$19.95
00694775 Bon Jovi – Slippery When Wet	$19.95
00694935 Boston: Double Shot Of Boston	$22.95
00694762 Cinderella – Heartbreak Station	$19.95
00692376 Cinderella – Long Cold Winter	$19.95
00692375 Cinderella – Night Songs	$19.95
00694875 Eric Clapton – Boxed Set	$75.00
00692392 Eric Clapton – Crossroads Vol. 1	$22.95
00692393 Eric Clapton – Crossroads Vol. 2	$22.95
00692394 Eric Clapton – Crossroads Vol. 3	$22.95
00690010 Eric Clapton – From The Cradle	$19.95
00660139 Eric Clapton – Journeyman	$19.95
00694869 Eric Clapton – Unplugged	$19.95
00692391 The Best of Eric Clapton	$19.95
00694896 John Mayall/Eric Clapton – Bluesbreakers	$19.95
00694873 Eric Clapton – Timepieces	$19.95
00694837 Albert Collins – The Complete Imperial Recordings	$19.95
00694862 Contemporary Country Guitar	$18.95
00660127 Alice Cooper – Trash	$19.95
00694941 Crash Test Dummies – God Shuffled His Feet	$19.95
00694840 Cream – Disraeli Gears	$19.95
00690033 Danzig – Prime Cuts	$19.95
00690007 Danzig 4	$19.95
00690034 Danzig	$18.95
00694844 Def Leppard – Adrenalize	$19.95
00660186 Alex De Grassi Guitar Collection	$19.95
00694831 Derek And The Dominos – Layla & Other Assorted Love Songs	$19.95
00692240 Bo Diddley Guitar Solos	$19.95
00660175 Dio – Lock Up The Wolves	$19.95
00660178 Willie Dixon	$24.95
00694915 Electric Blues Guitar Giants	$18.95
00694800 FireHouse	$18.95
00694867 FireHouse – Hold Your Fire	$19.95
00694920 Best of Free	$18.95

00694894 Frank Gambale – The Great Explorers	$19.95
00694807 Danny Gatton – 88 Elmira St	$19.95
00694848 Genuine Rockabilly Guitar Hits	$19.95
00694798 George Harrison Anthology	$19.95
00690068 Return of The Hellecasters	$19.95
00692930 Jimi Hendrix – Are You Experienced?	$19.95
00692931 Jimi Hendrix – Axis: Bold As Love	$19.95
00694944 Jimi Hendrix – Blues	$24.95
00660192 The Jimi Hendrix – Concerts	$24.95
00692932 Jimi Hendrix – Electric Ladyland	$24.95
00694923 Jimi Hendrix – The Experience Collection Boxed Set	$75.00
00660099 Jimi Hendrix – Radio One	$24.95
00694919 Jimi Hendrix – Stone Free	$19.95
00660024 Jimi Hendrix – Variations On A Theme: Red House	$19.95
00660029 Buddy Holly	$19.95
00660200 John Lee Hooker – The Healer	$19.95
00660169 John Lee Hooker – A Blues Legend	$19.95
00694850 Iron Maiden – Fear Of The Dark	$19.95
00694938 Elmore James – Master Electric Slide Guitar	$14.95
00694833 Billy Joel For Guitar	$19.95
00660147 Eric Johnson	$19.95
00694912 Eric Johnson – Ah Via Musicom	$19.95
00694911 Eric Johnson – Tones	$19.95
00694799 Robert Johnson – At The Crossroads	$19.95
00693186 Judas Priest – Metal Cuts	$19.95
00660226 Judas Priest – Painkiller	$19.95
00693187 Judas Priest – Ram It Down	$19.95
00693185 Judas Priest – Vintage Hits	$19.95
00694764 Kentucky Headhunters – Pickin' On Nashville	$19.95
00694795 Kentucky Headhunters – Electric Barnyard	$19.95
00660050 B. B. King	$19.95
00694903 The Best Of Kiss	$24.95
00694806 L.A. Guns – Hollywood Vampires	$18.95
00694794 Best Of Los Lobos	$18.95
00660199 The Lynch Mob – Wicked Sensation	$19.95
00694954 Lynyrd Skynyrd, New Best Of	$19.95
00660174 Yngwie Malmsteen – Eclipse	$19.95
00694845 Yngwie Malmsteen – Fire And Ice	$19.95
00694756 Yngwie Malmsteen – Marching Out	$19.95
00694755 Yngwie Malmsteen's Rising Force	$19.95
00660001 Yngwie Malmsteen – Rising Force – Odyssey	$19.95
00694757 Yngwie Malmsteen – Trilogy	$19.95
00694956 Bob Marley – Legend	$19.95
00690020 Meat Loaf – Bat Out Of Hell I & II	$22.95
00694952 Megadeth – Countdown To Extinction	$19.95
00694951 Megadeth – Rust In Peace	$22.95
00694953 Megadeth – Selections From "Peace Sells...But Who's Buying?" & "So Far, So Good...So What!"	$22.95
00692880 Metal Madness	$17.95
00694792 Metal Church – The Human Factor	$19.95
00694868 Gary Moore – After Hours	$19.95
00694849 Gary Moore – The Early Years	$19.95
00694802 Gary Moore – Still Got The Blues	$19.95
00694872 Vinnie Moore – Meltdown	$19.95
00694958 Mountain, Best Of	$19.95
00694895 Nirvana – Bleach	$19.95
00694913 Nirvana – In Utero	$19.95
00694883 Nirvana – Nevermind	$19.95
00690026 Nirvana – Unplugged In New York	$19.95
00694847 Best Of Ozzy Osbourne	$22.95
00694830 Ozzy Osbourne – No More Tears	$19.95
00694855 Pearl Jam – Ten	$19.95
00693800 Pink Floyd – Early Classics	$19.95
00693864 Police, The Best Of	$18.95

00692535 Elvis Presley	$18.95
00694975 Queen – Classic	$24.95
00694974 Queen – A Night At The Opera	$19.95
00694969 Queensryche – Selections from "Operation: Mindcrime"	$19.95
00694910 Rage Against The Machine	$19.95
00693910 Ratt – Invasion of Your Privacy	$19.95
00693911 Ratt – Out Of The Cellar	$19.95
00690027 Red Hot Chili Peppers – Out In L.A.	$19.95
00694968 Red Hot Chili Peppers – Selections from "What Hits!?"	$22.95
00694892 Guitar Style Of Jerry Reed	$19.95
00694899 REM – Automatic For The People	$19.95
00694898 REM – Out Of Time	$19.95
00660060 Robbie Robertson	$19.95
00694959 Rockin' Country Guitar	$19.95
00690014 Rolling Stones – Exile On Main Street	$24.95
00694976 Rolling Stones – Some Girls	$18.95
00694897 Roots Of Country Guitar	$19.95
00694836 Richie Sambora – Stranger In This Town	$19.95
00694805 Scorpions – Crazy World	$19.95
00694916 Scorpions – Face The Heat	$19.95
00694870 Seattle Scene	$18.95
00694885 Spin Doctors – Pocket Full Of Kryptonite	$19.95
00694962 Spin Doctors – Turn It Upside Down	$19.95
00694917 Spin Doctors – Up For Grabs	$19.95
00694796 Steelheart	$19.95
00694921 Steppenwolf, The Best Of	$22.95
00694801 Rod Stewart, Best Of	$22.95
00694957 Rod Stewart – Unplugged...And Seated	$22.95
00694180 Stryper – In God We Trust	$19.95
00694824 Best Of James Taylor	$16.95
00694846 Testament – The Ritual	$19.95
00694887 Thin Lizzy – The Best Of Thin Lizzy	$19.95
00694410 The Best of U2	$19.95
00694411 U2 – The Joshua Tree	$19.95
00660137 Steve Vai – Passion & Warfare	$24.95
00694904 Vai – Sex and Religion	$24.95
00694879 Stevie Ray Vaughan –In The Beginning	$19.95
00660136 Stevie Ray Vaughan – In Step	$19.95
00660058 Stevie Ray Vaughan – Lightnin' Blues 1983 – 1987	$24.95
00694835 Stevie Ray Vaughan – The Sky Is Crying	$19.95
00690015 Stevie Ray Vaughan – Texas Flood	$19.95
00690024 Stevie Ray Vaughan – Couldn't Stand The Weather	$19.95
00694776 Vaughan Brothers – Family Style	$19.95
00660196 Vixen – Rev It Up	$19.95
00694781 Warrant – Cherry Pie	$19.95
00694787 Warrant – Dirty Rotten Filthy Stinking Rich	$19.95
00694866 Warrant – Dog Eat Dog	$19.95
00694789 The Muddy Waters Guitar Collection	$24.95
00694888 Windham Hill Guitar Sampler	$18.95
00694786 Winger	$19.95
00694782 Winger – In The Heart Of The Young	$19.95
00694900 Winger – Pull	$19.95

Transcribed Scores are vocal and instrumental arrangements of music from some of the greatest groups in music. These excellent publications feature transcribed parts for lead vocals, lead guitar in notation and tablature, rhythm, guitar, bass, drums, and all of the various instruments used in each specific recording session. All songs are arranged exactly the way the artists recorded them.

THE BEATLES – THE BLUE BOOK

Can't Buy Me Love • Day Tripper • Here Comes The Sun • Hey Jude • Lady Madona • Penny Lane • Yesterday.
00674280 ....$14.95

THE BEATLES – THE YELLOW BOOK

A Day In The Life • Eight Days A Week • Eleanor Rigby • A Hard Day's Night • Hello, Goodbye • I Feel Fine • Something.
00673145 ....$14.95

THE BEATLES – THE GREEN BOOK

Come Together • Got To Get You Into My Life • I Saw Her Standing There • In My Life • Let It Be • Strawberry Fields Forever • Ticket To Ride.
00673395 ....$14.95

THE BEATLES – THE RED BOOK

All You Need Is Love • Back In The U.S.S.R. • Good Day Sunshine • The Long And Winding Road • Michelle • Paperback Writer • Please Please Me.
00675422 ....$14.95

THE BEST OF BLOOD SWEAT & TEARS

Seven hits from the quintessential jazz/rock group. Every note and nuance...vocal lines, brass, sax, keyboard, bass and drums, plus a synthesizer line for auxiliary instruments (each sound clearly identified). Features: And When I Die • God Bless The Child • Go Down Gamblin' • Lucretia MacEvil • Sometimes In Winter • Spinning Wheel • You've Made Me So Very Happy.
00673208 ....$18.95

THE BEST OF THE RIPPINGTONS

Exact transcriptions of the top songs from this cutting-edge jazz fusion group. Includes: Aspen • Curves Ahead • Indian Summer • Tourist In Paradise • and many more.
00673236 ....$18.95

THE BEST OF SHADOWFAX

This folio features fully-transcribed favorites from these jazzy Windham Hill recording artists. Songs include: Angel's Flight • The Dreams Of Children • Shadowdance • A Thousand Teardrops • and many more.
00699393......................$19.95

THE BEST OF SPYRO GYRA

A chronology of the favorite tunes from this award-winning jazz group. Note-for-note scores for sax, keyboards, mallets, guitar, bass, percussion/drums. 10 tunes including: Shaker Song • Morning Dance • Catching The Sun • Joy Ride.
00675170..........................$18.95

THE BEST OF STEELY DAN

10 songs from this highly acclaimed jazz/rock supergroup. Songs include: Reelin' In The Years • My Old School • Deacon Blues • Peg • Aja • Hey Nineteen.
00675200..........................$18.95

STING – TEN SUMMONER'S TALES

Complete scores to all 11 tracks on this album, including: Fields Of Gold • If I Ever Lose My Faith In You • It's Probably Me • and more.
00673230..........................$19.95

STING – NOTHING LIKE THE SUN

Matching folio to the popular LP by Sting, this collection contains complete instrument-for-instrument transcriptions for all 12 songs found on the album. Songs include: Be Still My Beating Heart • Englishman In New York • Straight To My Heart • and more.
00674655..........................$18.95

THE BEST OF TRAFFIC

Full scores from this band featuring Steve Winwood. 13 of their best, including: Dear Mr. Fantasy • Freedom Rider • Glad • Low Spark Of High-Heeled Boys • Paper Sun • and more.
00673227..........................$19.95

BEST OF WEATHER REPORT

A collection of 14 of their very best, including: Mysterious Traveller • Birdland • Palladium • Mr. Gone • Badia/Boogie Woogie Waltz Medley • Brown Street • 8:30.
00675520......................$18.95

YELLOW JACKETS – FOUR CORNERS

Complete instrument-for-instrument transcriptions for this Grammy Award-winning jazz/fusion group. Instrumentation includes keyboards, saxophone, bass and drums. Features all 10 tunes from the LP, including the hit "Mile High" and the bonus tune from the CD/cassette, "Indigo."
00675800......................$18.95

HAL•LEONARD

7777 W. BLUEMOUND RD. P.O. BOX 13819
MILWAUKEE, WISCONSIN 53213

Prices and availability subject to change

signature licks

FINALLY! A series that helps the guitar player gain invaluable insight into the styles and techniques of the greatest players of today! The Signature Licks book/audio packs are especially formatted to give you instruction on how to play a particular artist style by using the actual transcribed, "right from the record" licks! Designed for use by anyone from beginner right up to the experienced player who is looking to expand his insight. The books contain full performance notes and an overview of each artist or group's style with transcriptions in notes and tab. The audio features playing tips and techniques as well as playing examples at a slower tempo.

The Best Of Eric Clapton
Learn to play 12 of his greatest, including: After Midnight • Cocaine • Forever Man • Lay Down Sally • White Room.

00673390 Book/Cassette Pack.................$17.95
00699339 Book/CD Pack.........................$19.95

The Best Of Def Leppard
A step-by-step breakdown of the band's guitar styles and techniques featuring songs from four albums. The audio accompaniment presents each song in a stereo split with full band backing. Songs include: Bringin' On The Heartbreak • Hysteria • Photograph • and more.
00696516 Book/CD Pack........................$19.95
00696515 Book/Cassette Pack................$17.95

Eric Johnson
Learn the nuances of technique and taste that make Eric Johnson unique among guitarists. On this pack's 60-minute audio supplement, Wolf Marshall explores both the theoretical and hands-on aspects of Eric Johnson's best recorded work. It also comprehensively explores: Hybrid picking • String-skipping • Motivic development • Scale-combining • Position shifting • and additional aspects of his playing that makes him one of the most admired guitarists today. Some of his best songs are examined, including: Trademark • Cliffs Of Dover • Song For George • and more.
00699317 Book/CD Pack................$19.95
00699318 Book/Cassette Pack.........$17.95

The Best Of Kiss
by Jeff Perrin
Learn the trademark riffs and solos behind one of rock's most legendary bands. This pack includes a hands-on analysis of 12 power house classics, including: Deuce • Strutter • Rock And Roll All Nite • Detroit Rock City • and more.
00699412 Book/Cassette Pack................$17.95
00699413 Book/CD Pack.........................$19.95

George Lynch
Super-charge your licks using this, in-depth analysis of the guitar playing of George Lynch, with music and tab. Lynch's trademark wide-stretch fingerings, two-handed tapping, and legato techniques are fully explained and annotated. Learn scale-combining, voice leading, symmetrical melodic shapes, orchestration with rhythm guitar, and more, as George applies them in his unique and fiery recordings. The book examines 7 of Lynch Mob's songs, including: Wicked Sensation • All I Want • Sweet Sister Mercy • and more. Includes 44-minute audio supplement demonstrating each technique.
00699314 Book/Cassette Pack.......................$17.95
00699313 Book/CD Pack..............................$19.95

The Guitars Of Elvis
by Wolf Marshall
Elvis' music is synonymous with the birth of rock and roll and the invention of rock guitar. Wolf Marshall takes you back to the roots where it all started with this exploration into the influential style of the King's fretmen. This book is a step-by-step breakdown of the playing techniques of Scotty Moore, Hank Garland, and James Burton. Players will learn their unique concepts and techniques by studying this special collection of Elvis' greatest guitar-driven moments. The 75-minute accompanying audio presents each song in stereo-split with full band backing. Songs include: A Big Hunk O' Love • Heartbreak Hotel • Hound Dog • Jailhouse Rock • See See Rider • and more!
00696508 Book/Cassette Pack.......................$17.95
00696507 Book/CD Pack..............................$19.95

Steve Vai
Play along with the actual backing tracks from *Passion and Warfare* and *Sex and Religion* especially modified by Steve Vai himself! Learn the secrets behind a guitar virtuoso then play along like the pro himself.
00673248 Book/Cassette Pack.......................$19.95
00673247 Book/CD Pack..............................$22.95

Stevie Ray Vaughan
by Wolf Marshall
This book takes you on an in-depth exploration of this guitar genius by examining various aspects of Vaughan's playing. Marshall explains his influences, tuning, equipment, picking technique and other aspects of Vaughan's sound. In addition, he transcribes, in notes and tab, parts of 13 of Vaughan's most famous songs, and explains how they were played and what makes them so unique. The 59-minute accompanying cassette or CD includes samples of the parts of the songs being examined. A must for any serious Vaughan fan or aspiring guitarist!
00699315 Book/Cassette Pack.......................$17.95
00699316 Book/CD Pack..............................$19.95

Prices, contents, and availability subject to change without notice. Some products may not be available outside the U.S.A.

FOR MORE INFORMATION, SEE YOUR LOCAL MUSIC DEALER, OR WRITE TO:

HAL•LEONARD
CORPORATION
7777 W. BLUEMOUND RD. P.O. BOX 13819 MILWAUKEE, WI 53213